The Wrong Way Round

Being the (mis)adventures of Sgt. Pepsi and Miss Mavis Ming on board NB Hekla (græna þröngt báturinn[0])

[0] The closest I could get to Icelandic[1] for Green Narrow boat
[1] On account of Hekla being an Icelandic active Volcano[2]
[2] Or an old Norse name for the Gateway to Hell

Contents

Well, yes, this book does have contents.

It even has chapter headings.

But I couldn't be bothered to go through the manuscript and list them - anyway the page numbers will probably jump about all over the place.

Best to treat it as a bit of a mystery tour and find out as you go along

OK?

This page intentionally left blank
Well, it would be blank if I hadn't type the above.

Tonight's Smoking Room View

I live in a dream world of reflections.

"Tonight's smoking room view.
No camera can do justice to this.
I stand at the back of Hekla; it is like living on the surface of a mirror.
The trees reflected in the glass-smooth surface of the still waters.
In the near distance a ridge, festooned with a garland of orange and white lights.
Sometimes a cruise is like a grand tour of England's back gardens, the scruffy, the ordinary, and the fabulous.
But I would not exchange our ever changing view of their back gardens with their static view of our canal.
We really are living the dream, and I sometimes pity those who can not share in our un-reality."

Imagine, if you will, - if you live in a house with a small pond in your garden, that you live in a small house floating in your garden pond, Well, we live in a house, floating in a garden pond. - but the pond is in Britain's back garden - a 2,500-ish mile long pond in the back garden of England. <If you don't have a garden pond, or if you have no imagination, then perhaps best to let your eyes slide down this paragraph and pretend I didn't write it.>

One of the advantages of being a smoker whose wife is a non-smoker, hence being barred from smoking in the home, is that you have to retreat to the outside to have a ciggie.

But we live on a narrowboat, furthermore a narrowboat without a home mooring, thus making us what is termed Continuous Cruisers. Most of the time, 'outside' is not like popping out into the back garden, especially on a dark, cold winters night, when 'outside' might mean standing on a very muddy towpath in the rain.

So the answer is to sit on the step just inside the open doors of the engine room, with the door to the inside of the boat firmly shut. This means that periodically through the evening, I get to sit getting my nicotine & tar fix whilst gazing out into the night.

I discovered this illicit pleasure on the first night of living on our new home, the narrowboat Hekla, moored at Norbury in rural Staffordshire, where we had bought her in January that first year of becoming water gypsies.

The air was crisp, not a breath of wind stirred the surface of the canal. Frost was in the air, and the silhouette reflections of the trees contrasted with the warm light spilling from the Navigation Inn, and the sparse street lights and spotlights of the boatyard, all perfectly reflected in the glass-smooth surface of the cut.

It didn't do much for any attempts at giving up the weed. I kept looking forward to the next ciggie so that I could sit on the back step inside the smoking room, and lose myself in the hypnotic beauty before me.

And I started taking photos and posting them on social media, with the title "Tonight's smoking room view." And thus an internet meme was born.

So where did it begin?

Go back far enough and I suppose I was smitten with boats on a couple of Norfolk Broads holidays with a gang of mates - wonderful times. From what I can remember in between pubs.

Then I got married, and the next boating fix was our first ever narrowboat hire, on what to us was a *huge* 48ft long narrowboat *Menna*, with me, Lesley, her sister Gillian and our 2 Old English Sheepdogs, Emma and Ben in the summer of 1983

They had produced a litter of 6 adorable puppies - and after the hard work of helping raise them (Emma was a terrible mum - we had to hold her down so that they could feed from her - but Ben was an absolute model father, even helping carry the pups into Emma's box at feeding time) we sold them on to new families and the proceeds paid for our weeks much needed holiday.

We had a thoroughly enjoyable time - even when we had the inevitable break-down (well, break-up, I suppose, because the engine would not stop that night, so after a lot of head scratching I finally found the fuel feed tap and cut the fuel off)

I think Emma and Ben enjoyed it at least as much as we did. We set off from the hire base outside Chester, and cruised down to Hurleston Junction, and onto the Llangollen canal. One day we were on the back deck cruising along when suddenly there was a splash. Ben had fallen in off the bow. We cut the engine and as we drifted on he swam the length of the boat and I reached down and hoiked him up onto the boat - he shook himself (thanks for that.) looked at us with a delighted grin on his face, jumped through the rear doors, down the length of the boat and Dove Off The Front. Three times he did this before we shut the front doors to stop him. Meanwhile we were causing mayhem with the other boaters, who were laughing so much at his antics they were crashing into the banks and each other.

The next doggie adventure came at Grindley Brook. I was working the locks, and opened one bottom gate and stepped the 3ft across to the other gate and Emma decided to follow me. Her front legs landed OK - her back legs pounding the air for a few seconds then Splosh. In she went. She immediately swam to the lock wall and desperately and futilely scrabbled at it to climb up it. No amount of shouting or cajoling could induce her to swim out of the open lock so that we could lift her out at the bank, so I had to put on my Tarzan head and clamber down the beams of the lock gate - when she finally twigged and swam over to me.

I was waist deep in bloody cold canal water (the Llangollen canal is fed directly off the River Dee at Horseshoe Falls above Llangollen) and with 60lbs of soaking wet Old English Sheep Dog trying to climb up me.

We then did what was probably one of the most stupid things in my life. Lesley got onto Menna and brought her into the lock. Somehow I managed to throw Emma into the bows and leapt in after her as the boat came into the lock gates - the clearance between a 20 ton steal narrowboat and the lock walls is around 6 inches. It could have hurt. A Lot. And I would find out just how much it could hurt 32 years later.

So our first narrowboat holiday drew to a reluctant close. It was dramatic at times (the Pontcysylte and Chirk Aqueducts), adventurous, and at times dramatic - and we were bitten by the canal bug. It had proved to be a much more interesting time than cruising the rivers of Norfolk, with the locks and lift bridges adding to the fun, as well as the fascinating and ever changing scenery, the sense of history and the industrial archaeology and heritage you are soaked in.

Fast forward 3 decades, we had 3 young adult children, Vicky, Ross and Mike. I was self employed with my own small 2-man-band software company, Vicky was finishing off at Lincoln University, having spent every summer at kids camps in the USA and had a job lined up - Lesley had just graduated with a

2.1 in Fine Arts at Sheffield Hallam as a mature student (where she went 'by accident' - but that's another story) - savings were down a lot having put both of them through Uni for the past 4 years. Ross had left home and was living with his partner, Mike was still a home boy but had a reasonably steady job (if you can call a Zero-Hours contract steady.) and we were rattling around in a 4 bedroom house. (Well, it was a 5 bedroom house when we bought it, but we knocked through from the master bedroom into the cupboard that was laughably referred to as the small bedroom to make a walk-in-dressing room.)

So we started thinking about down sizing. We had loved boating and the canals for many years, and had friends who lived on narrowboats, but it was the financial crash in 2007 that was the catalyst. Vicky's job lined up for when she returned from her last summer teaching American kids horse riding fell though. Many of my customers began cutting back and business slowed dramatically, then Ross lost his job and turned up with his (then) partner in tow, along with a 7ft Boa Constrictor, 3 lizards, a pair of white rats, and a trio of manic Russian Gerbils.

Vicky, being Vicky, claimed the 2nd double bedroom for herself. Ross & Menagerie moved into the 3rd double room, and the smallest bedroom had been converted to my home office, so poor Mike, the youngest, was left with the couch to sleep on.

Eventually Vicky found a job in Lincoln and got a rented flat there. Ross found another job in Newark and found a flat there, leaving Lesley, Mike and myself - so we decided that we would down-size to a narrowboat. Then the kids could not move back in again.

So the house went on the market - and sat there for 4 years. We started looking at boats, buying the boating magazines and poring over the adverts, visiting marinas and brokerages and dreaming of the day when we would have our own floating home. Very frustrating, and we saw boat after boat that we would have loved get sold. However the time was not wasted and we did a **lot** of homework on living afloat.

Then one day in November a dapper chap knocked on our door and asked if we had considered selling the house at auction? I said "No chance. We're not **that** desperate." But he went on to explain that we did not have to accept any bid, we set out minimum, and that would be the reserve. If there were no bids at or above that, it would not sell. All the buyers are pre-qualified, and the winning bidder pays a 10% non-refundable deposit, and completion takes place in 28 days.

So we though what the heck, give it a go. And it came to pass a few weeks later we attended the auction in a posh hotel, and as hour house came up we stood on tenterhooks as the bidding opened - and we sold.   After waiting for 4 years we were faced with being homeless in 4 *weeks*.

We have a Cunning Plan [tm]

Given that we had been looking at boats for 4 years, we anticipated a long search for our boat to find us. (In boating circles, it is generally accepted that 'the boat finds you') so Plan A was devised, and we scoured the free adds and internet to find a cheap caravan that we could put on our daughters garden as accommodation and a base to continue our boat search in earnest.

We found one for sale, charmingly described as a "future classic" for the reasonable price of £400 not too far away in South Yorkshire, so we drove over to meet with a very nice young divorced single mother who was sad to sell it but needed cash to pay for urgent car repairs. They had used it for festivals, Glastonbury and the like, and she was a little apologetic about the interior décor - which was very new-age, with a purple gossamer cloth across the ceiling and Indian inspired drapes and cushions - she made an apologetic remark about it not being to our taste, what with us being 'oldies' - and I said "Young lady, my generation *invented* your culture." which brought a smile, if not a chuckle.

Anyway, the deal was done, and we arranged a day to come and collect it - with one *minor* problem of not having a car with a tow bar. Happily one of my customers obligingly loaned me a land rover for the job, and so we towed our new temporary home to our daughter's house in Lincolnshire, so we had somewhere to go come the planned completion date of 18th January.

We actually had a little more time on our side as the 4 week timetable was 4 *working* weeks, so with the Xmas break we had more like 6 weeks to organise ourselves, and decide what to do with a 4 bedroom house full of 'stuff' and nowhere to move it to.

We had actually been 'downsizing' for the 4 years since we decided to move onto a narrowboat - we must have re-stocked every charity shop in the nearby towns and villages, as well as being on first name terms with the blokes at the local recycling place - but still every room, the garage and the attic were full to bursting.

There is a newsgroup I frequent, UK.Rec.Sheds - an odd place, and nothing to do with sheds at all, but we have a name for this stuff, Tat - in 3 levels: Low Quality Tat (LQT - which might include such things as old paint tins with brushes set hard in them, jam jars full of assorted screws and nails); Medium Quality Tat (MQT - which may be things like broken stuff that could be fixed, or cannibalised for bits that might cumin andy at some point); and Top Quality Tat (TQT - which may be books, working tools, computer parts, ornaments etc.)

LQT goes to the skip - with a wrench, obviously. MQT is generally divided up into skip-fodder or charity shop fodder, while TQT is offered to the kids for their respective homes, or earmarked for storage. We contacted a local storage company and negotiated a deal for a room about the size of our garage, and the hire of a Luton van to do the moving of this stuff, which had already commenced using the car to transport spare bedding, clothes etc. To the caravan at our daughter's house about an hours drive away.

We also started moving what MQT & TQT we could fit into my car, an Alfa 156 Sportwagon (Alfa Romeo do *not* make estate cars.) and arranged the hire van for the day before D Day to move the rest, furniture etc. into storage, or the items our kids wanted to their respective houses.

Then, like all plans, it unravelled.

We had for some time now given up on going to view boats - it was frustrating finding boats we liked and could afford only to see them sold under us. We even had originally planned to find ourselves a mooring, and went so far as to put a bid in on one on the Canal & River Trust auction site. In Shireoaks Marina, on the Chesterfield canal near Worksop, which happened to be about 400 yards from my small software company's serviced office. Fortunately we were out-bid and didn't get it - otherwise we would have been forking out £2,500 for nothing.

But now we had a definite date when we knew we could purchase, so the week before Christmas 2013 we pencilled in 3 boats to go and view. First and favourite was called Badger, located at Great Haywood marina on the Trent and Mersey canal in Staffordshire. It was a 'proper' Trad style boat with a traditional boatman's cabin at the stern, complete with boatman's stove, drop down bed and multi-function cupboard/table, then an engine room with a gleaming Russell Newbury engine, then the permanent bedroom - looking very cosy, like an olde worlde cottage box bed, then a small bathroom (shower, toilet, sink) a small but complete galley, and a reasonably sized main cabin with settee and small table & 2 chars.

Perfect. A bit towards the top end of the budget we had set, but affordable. Then we had a rummage and came across the last hull survey - which said that she would likely need some over-plating in the near future due to hull pitting. That made it a no-go for us.

So we left it and headed of to 2nd choice, a boat we had found on Apollo Duck web site, at Industrial Narrowboats at Streethay on the Shropshire union canal.
This looked perfect on paper (although it did not boast an engine room as Badger had) with 300W of solar panels and a 7KVA 240V generator.

It was a disaster area. Inside was so dark - almost black. Offset by a rug in the middle of the floor with shocking pink polka-dots, and a range of kitchenware in the galley of all shades of fluorescent greens yellows and pinks. The bathroom looked like a 1950's pre-fab, all in all a total wreck. We later bumped into a chap who had bought it nearly 2 years after we had turned it down - he was a complete novice and was full of horror stories of mechanical breakdowns and water leaks.

We had a fall-back, a boat we had seen several times in the adverts, but it didn't really appeal to us, but it was just up the road at Norbury Wharf, there were enough hours in the day, so we trundled along in a sort of resigned pessimism to view it.

By the time we got there the heavens opened and there was a full downpour. The helpful Simon in the brokerage gave us keys to several boats in our price range to look at, and we boarded each before our intended viewing - all proved to be unwelcoming, cold, uninviting boats, so we finally ended up on the gleaming green (because of the heavy rain.) Hekla - and instantly fell in love with her.

Lesley and I were like 2 school kids wandering around wide eyed - we flicked a light switch and the inset ceiling spotlight came on. "Look. The lights work." - then we spotted the radio/CD player glowing blue LEDs in the side of the cabinet by the front of the saloon. Diagonal honey-coloured tongue and groove walls, contrasting dark wood beams in the roof, shiny newly fitted galley with black work surfaces and black fridge and built-in cooker. Stable-doors at the bows, a separate bunk bedroom, neat and compact bathroom with ceramic flush toiled and walk-in shower stall, and a very comfy looking bed at the stern.

We sat in the black leather captains chairs and sat smiling at our surroundings, the essential multi-fuel stove sitting on a tiled plinth in the corner, and each other. It looked like our boat had found us. Simon came over and sang the praises of the Lister engine, and started it up - it was like music to our ears. A Proper boat engine. Albeit in a 'trad-style' engine room and boxed in under the floor. It even had a nice black plate with Lister-Petter highlighted in gold lettering.

Back in the office and we told Simon we were very interested, but had vowed not to part with any cash until we had the funds in our account in mid January. He was very understanding, but said there was no way he could hold it for us if another buyer came along with a deposit, using a bit of salesman's license in saying that although this was the week before Xmas, there were plenty of buyers looking over the holidays.

We said we would be in touch and took our leave for the 150 mile dark and rainy drive home, the subject of our anguished conversation being whether to risk a deposit or not - and could we raise the £1000 at all.

At home, all over the weekend we agonised over it, but Hekla had stolen our hearts, and we managed to rustle up the necessary cash and on the Monday I phoned Simon. People had repeatedly told us *never* to pay the asking price, and many said "Put in a silly low offer first and negotiate up from that"

When we had initially seen Hekla advertised several months previously the asking price was £45k - but it dropped twice in the intervening period before we viewed her to £35k. Simon had told us that there was a bit of a tragedy behind it, as a couple who owned it were in the process of 'doing it up' to live aboard full time, but the husband had suddenly dropped dead, and his widow had walked into Norbury, being the nearest brokerage, and said "Get rid of it"

So I made my first 'silly' offer of £25k which was laughed at. "£30k is more likely" so we spent a jolly half hour ping-ponging offers and counter offers, before finally agreeing on £27.5k subject to survey, which we were happy with as it was well within our budget. So the next day, 23rd December we drove back over to Norbury for a second viewing - again Hekla was all shiny bright - yes, it was raining heavily again. We arranged a price and date for Hekla to be put into the dry dock for the full survey and, if satisfactory, blacking the hull. (something that is done about every 3 years to a steel narrowboat hull)

Simon gave us a name of a surveyor that the boatyard use, and we contacted him for a price and availability, but also thought it prudent to find another independent surveyor, which we did - and he was willing to do the job on the Sunday we had provisionally booked for Hekla to be in dry dock.

So back home to spend the next 2 weeks in excited anticipation and frantic planning for moving out of our house on the date fixed for exchange, as well as further exhausting attempts to reduce the amount of Low, Medium and High Quality Tat we would either take with us, donate to the kids, drop off at local charity shops or consign to the skips at the local recycling centre.

Xmas was a full family affair spent at our daughter's house in Lincolnshire - we slept in our caravan, our 2 sons on the couches. We had our 3 dogs Max, Tilly and Benson with us also, and Vicky had her greyhound Roxy, and Ross had his white Staffie Jezza. Which was a bit of a problem since earlier in the year we had been out walking them in a local woods, Jezza getting on fine with our 3, until he started being a bit amorous with Tilly - Benson's mum. And Benson was having none of it and they had a real set-to with each other, which Ross and I managed to break up with a heck of a struggle - and from that day on Benson and Jezza are mortal enemies.

And so on Boxing Day, after managing to keep them apart in separate rooms all over Xmas, Jezza managed to force his was past someone opening the lounge door and they went at it hammer and tongs.   Jezza had Bensons mouth in the typical Staffie jaw-clamp and we could not get his mouth open. I had a horrid thought that someone had once said that the only way to get a Staffie to release his grip was to stick your hand up his arse.

Nofa Ixta Boda[1]

The day we completed the sale was drawing ever closer. Despite massive efforts to de-clutter we still had what seemed to be exactly the same amount of 'stuff' as we had before we started. I had already started moving some of the 'stuff' into storage, and on D day -1 we collected the Luton van and set about moving the bulkier items of furniture into storage - a task not helped by our remaining live at home son Mike who, despite all the evidence to the contrary, was still in denial about the fact that we were moving out. So no help there then.

We had discussed all of this with our youngest son repeatedly, and even included provision for him in our ideal boat (in this case the single bunk room) but he was still in his own dream world where we lived happily ever after in the house he was born in. (well, he was born in hospital, but you know what I mean.)

After several trips it became obvious that we would need more time. We negotiated another day's van hire, and even so, on D-Day, the appointed time of 2:00 p.m., we still had a shedload of 'stuff' still to deal with. Panic set in. Fortunately the buyers lived in the village and were very understanding. Their intention was to convert our 4 bedroom house into a 3 apartment shared rental house, and would be taking a while before starting work.

Even so, we were still moving stuff late into the night, the final exhausted run was to our daughter's house in Lincolnshire, returning the rental van eventually (only a day late.) the next morning - and we were now officially living in our little 'future classic' touring caravan - in January.

A couple of days later we set off again to Norbury to meet up with Michael Clarke, our chosen surveyor, to discover if Hekla passed his scrutiny and we had a new floating home to move onto.

A full survey is not *essential* when you buy a boat, but just like buying a house, it is a little foolish not to have one done. Also in the case of boats over a certain age an out-of-water hull survey is a requirement for most insurance companies. Another bit of legislation you have to comply with is the dreaded BSS - Boat Safety Scheme - similar to a car MOT, but only required every 4 years. Hekla had just under 2 years before the previous BSS expired, but Michael suggested that he could include a new 4 year 'ticket' at a knock down price if we had that done with the full hull and valuation survey.

We arrived by mid-morning to find Michael well into his job, Hekla was in the covered dry dock, and not out in the rain. This was brought home to us by the fact that on our previous 2 visits Hekla was bright and shiny green - but undercover in the dry she was showing her 23 years age and the paintwork was a bit dull. But she was still an impressive sight, as we stood in the bottom of the dock and walked around her hull inspecting it, the view of the bows towing over us was reminiscent of a Viking longship prow. Upswept and gracefully curved in 3 dimensions.

Michael came down to meet us and walked us around the hull showing us the chalk marks where he had taken the ultrasonic thickness readings, and pointing out the only area of minor concern where the bottom plate overlap was ground down from the recommended 12mm to 8 mm at the turn in at the stern - a common wear pattern on narrowboats as this is the part of the hull most likely to make contact with the canal bank when mooring up. Nothing of great concern, but he recommended that we ask to boatyard to weld on some 'D' bars on both sides while Hekla was out of the water and being blacked. A little minor wear in the rudder bottom bearing - again something we asked the boatyard to sort while she was in dock.

Back up on deck and Michael gave us a brief walk around the boat, pointing out any possible concerns and giving us an idea of what the various switches, knobs and controls did. There were a half dozen or so very minor issues to be sorted for the new BSS - a fuse, another fire extinguisher and a fire blanket, and the bow-thruster battery to be better secured in its box in the bow side pod. We agreed to have these done and he said he would issue the new BSS when we sent him a copy of the receipt for the works done by the boatyard.

Overall he said we had a good sound boat. Hekla's hull was of 10-6-4 construction. A 10mm base plate, 6mm main hull sides, and 4mm cabin walls and roof. Maximum pitting on base plate and hull sides was under 1mm in all but two spots, well within 'acceptable limits' As to valuation - valuing a narrowboat is about as accurate as valuing a house on land. Get 3 estate agents and they will give 3 totally different numbers. However he asked what we were paying and when we told him he was surprised, and said "For that price you could live on it for 5 years and still get more than your money back." Which was OK by us.

He also commented, in passing, that the bathroom door was hidden behind the ex-toilet door. We hadn't even noticed that there was no door on the bathroom. Next door was originally a separate toilet, complete with olde fashioned Engaged type lock (brass, of course) - which we now call The Utility Room - i.e. where we store the washing machine and throw all the other tat we have wanting a home. The bathroom door had, for some reason known only to the previous owners, been removed and shoved behind the inward-opening door.

Anyway, that aside, off we toddled to the office to shake hands on the deal, arrange for the required additional works to be done and the hull re-blacked, and sort out the full purchase price, less deposit, paid by bank transfer - and within a week we would be the new owners of Hekla, our new floating home.

Back to the caravan. So excited. Our dream from our 20's and for the past 4 years was finally happening.

The weeks wait seemed to go on forever. But the day dawned (raining, as to be expected) and we set off with the first car load of 'stuff' to Hekla - the first of a week and more of daily commutes from Lincolnshire to Norbury with the Alfa loaded to the roof with bedding, clothing, kitchen stuff………

Another problem. The Alfa started playing up. (Shut up at the back there. It's an Alfa Romeo - it has *Character*.) The clutch got progressively stiffer and stiffer, the gears crashing in 1st and reverse. A call to a local Alfa specialist revealed a new clutch and labour would set us back over £600 - and a 7 to 10 day wait for parts and a slot in the workshop.

The car was 10 years old, and to be honest, not worth a lot more than the cost of the repair. As luck would have it we spotted an advert in Autotrader for a Mazda 626 local private sale in Lincoln for £450 12 months tax and MOT included. No Brainer. We arranged to see it and have a test drive. The seller was a very nice old chap - a Hungarian Refugee from the 1960's uprising. Recently diagnosed with diabetes, and his diving license suspended. He said he had owned the car as 2nd owner from new, only just had the MOT done and it had done a whopping 150 miles in the year since the previous MOT. Deal done, the Alfa put on a famous auction site as 'spares or repair' I was sad to see it go, I love Alfas, and that 156 had served me well for over 3 years. The Mazda was older, and in good condition, nice to drive, but, well, a bit dull compared to an Alfa Romeo. But needs must, and we continued our long distance move onto Hekla.

And eventually we spent our first night on board our new home. 1st priority was to sort out some wood for the stove. A bag of kiln dried cut logs from the chandlery was bought and like a pair of demented children we lit our first 'real' fire in - I don't know how long.

Sitting in the cabin on a dark and frosty January night, we sat for hours just watching the flames flickering behind the glass door, occasionally stirring to add a couple of logs to the blaze - basking in the warmth, not only from the fire, but sat in our wood-lined cocoon with the rich warm honey coloured walls and ceiling adding to the overall feeling of contentment, and firmly establishing in our minds that we had made the right decision to sell up and move onto the boat.

Our house had been heated by LPG central heating, and the nearest we got to an open fire for over 20 years was the coal effect gas fire, and the heating at times was strictly rationed because the cost of LPG went through the roof - especially when we had to switch from a bulk tank to 47Kg gas bottles. We used to have a 'budget account' - payments spread over the year, and the tank was automatically topped up every 2 weeks in winter - until one day a few years ago we ran out. A call to our suppliers Shell Gas was a little annoying to say the least. "Oh. Has no one told you? Health and Safety rules have changed, and the tanker driver has to be able to see the tanker from the tank, and that's not possible in your installation"

To describe the following conversation as a 'Free And Frank Exchange OF Views' would be an understatement - and after my rant calmed down a little, the manager was summoned to the phone and they accepted they had let us down, and to compensate they said they would remove the 2,000 litre tank from the back garden *at no charge to us* . **WHAT?** and install a change-over valve system and 2 pairs of 47Kg gas bottles - with a little push they agreed to no charge for the gas either. But that then left us with the problem of the cost being *much* higher than bulk gas, and no budget account to spread the cost over the year, and at one point we were paying well over £200 a month just to keep the house above freezing. And augmenting it with electric heating hiked our electricity bill even further.

So the warm glow from the stove, so comforting after those chilled winters was such a satisfaction. But one tinged with a bit of an issue. We were warm as toast sat in out chairs, but the feet were a bit on the chilly side, and as soon as we stood up our heads went into a sauna-like wave of heat near the ceiling. The stove was in the front of the boat, and the heat did make its way down the boat to our bedroom in the stern - just. So we had to start up the Alde gas central heating as well - a small, efficient boiler and just 2 radiators, one in the bedroom and one half way down the corridor.

We had heard of Eco Fans before - rather pricey when we looked, but being a scrooge at heart, I found one on a well known on-line auction site for less than half the price we had seen them for in chandlers. The principle is very simple - if you casually ignore the science behind the Peltier chip. Such a chip will generate a small electrical current if one side is heated and the other side cooled - or vice versa, if you apply a current one side warms up and the other side cools. They are mounted sandwiched between a heavy metal base and metal cooling fins above, you sit them on top of the stove, and when they heat up, they spin. And the result was astonishing. The cold-feet-hot-head issue disappeared, and the warm air was also gently wafted down the boat. We only needed to light the gas central heating in extremely cold weather.

Our son Ross, being an inquisitive and inventive lad, was fascinated, so he ordered a peltier chip on line for £1, a 6 volt motor, and a model aeroplane propeller, clamped the chip between a lump of metal and an old computer CPU cooling fin and made a perfectly functional working one for under a tenner.

When we bought Hekla the wharf included 2 weeks free moorings - but this was directly opposite the wharf outside the Navigation Inn. Fine, but there is this thing called the "Shroppie Shelf" - a stone projection just a few inches below the water line, sticking out over a foot from the bank. It is not all along the canal, but is quite common, and the outside of the Navigation was such a place. Couple with the fact that the grassy bank down from the pub was steep, and in January somewhat muddy and slippery, and with 3 dogs who would be *bound* to fall into the gap (not to mention one of us after a beer or 3 in the pub.) that the next day we decided to move Hekla up the canal a bit onto a more stable mooring on the towpath north of the junction.

One small problem though. Hekla was pointing South - in the wrong direction. Also we had no idea how much fuel was in the tank, nor how much fresh water was in the water tank. We were far from boating novices, but we had not so much as touched a tiller in anger for nearly 2 years. And Hekla was a new (to us) boat, and all boats have their own little foibles and quirks, so our maiden voyage on Hekla was about 50 yards. From one side of the junction basin to the other to fill up with diesel and water, and also to turn her around so that she was pointing in the direction we wanted to go.

It is an un-written rule of life on a narrowboat, a tradition, or an old charter or something, but whenever you have spectators watching you (known to us boat people as Gongoozlers) *Something will go wrong.* and we had plenty of gongoozlers both outside the pub, and on our destination, the wharf opposite. So of course it all went perfectly. *Not.* Lots of shouts of encouragement from all sides, and the old bloke on the wharf waiting for us was shouting destructions at us "Tiller This Way." "No - the Other Way" "More throttle." and so on - but we did eventually manage our 33-point turn, rewarded with some cheering and a ripple of applause from the drunken locals lining the balcony at the pub.

So job jobbed. Our first diesel fill up - 113 Litres and £90 to the poorer, filled the water tank, and added a bag of smokeless fuel to the bill (the bag of logs lasted a whole day.) and we set off for our second slightly jaded-maiden voyage of another 100 yards or so, through a narrow bridge and up the towpath to tie up on rings and a bank that was, if not un-muddy, at least was flat and level with the side of the boat. And so our second night afloat passed in blissful warmth and general all round smug cosiness. That night we even had a sharp frost, and again, the inner child had us both oohing and aahing at the white sparkly stuff on Hekla's roof.

We decided to spend the next day where we were and acclimatise ourselves with the boat and our new life - also sorting out unpacking, who had first dibs on the wardrobes and drawers (Lesley) and generally taking stock of our new home. And taking stock was a short affair indeed. The sum total of our boating equipment amounted to an aged and suspect 10 ft barge pole on the roof, and ….. well, that was it.

There is an awful lot of ironmongery required to navigate a narrowboat around our 2,500 - ish miles of inland waterways, and a bewildering array of variations on a theme for these things. Essentially you have to have a windlass (at least 2 - because if you only have one, sure as eggs is eggs you will drop it in a lock.) Then you have to have some means of mooring the boat up in the wilds where there are no mooring rings. There are a variety of Mooring Pins - basically huge tent pegs, and a lump hammer to hammer them into the sometimes soft, sometimes concrete hard ground by the canal. Where there are 'pilings' - just like the Armco on motorways, you need either 'nappy pins' - so called because they look like, well, a huge nappy pin. And/or Chains - a 2ft length of steel chain with a big ring on one end, and a smaller ring on the other - you dangle the end with the small ring down into the water behind the piling, then kneel down in the usually wet and/or muddy bank to stick your hand in the water to lift it up the other side and thread it though the bigger ring, then pass your mooring rope through the little ring and thus tie your boat securely to the bank.

Then you need a special key called, depending on where you are, a 'Water Conservation Key' in parts posh, or an Anti Vandal key in less salubrious locations - it's basically a box spanner with a square hole in the end. You also need a 'BW Watermate Key' (still called such, even in this modern age where British Waterways had been transmogrified into the Canal and River Trust (CaRT)) which grants you access to the hallowed service areas around the system, which at best are buildings with toilets, showers, and Elsan disposal points, at worst (more commonly) a dodgy looking toilet and, if you are lucky, and indoor Elsan disposal point, or if you are unlucky, a grotty oversized urinal with a low brick wall around it. Which can be a bit of a bugger if the sound of the effluent gurgling into the bowl and subsequent hosing and rinsing of the toilet cassette brings on a sudden and *urgent* need to have a wee!

As we were intending to go to the Chesterfield Canal, and this involves navigating the tidal and non-tidal mighty river Trent, we also need an anchor. And not just *any* anchor either. There is a whole complicated and befuddling rigmarole of types, sizes, and weights to choose from, and a lump of chain of a certain weight and length, and a pretty hefty and long length of rope. All of which, if you listen to the various 'experts' on the interweb, have to be *exactly* right or you will surely sink and drown to death.

Or - you ask at the boatyard if they have any second hand ones, and stump up £70 for a hefty glorified folding grappling hook complete with 'some' chain, and 'some' rope.

So laden down with several hundredweight of assorted and diverse ironmongery we staggered back to Hekla so that now we would have some actual stock to take stock of. - Oh. I nearly forgot. You also simply *have* to have a boat hook. Preferably one with a brass (of if you are not of the Brasso persuasion a Chrome Plated) hook and pointy thing on the end of your 6 foot stout pole. Wandering down the towpath with this implement carried at a jaunty angle over your shoulder, you feel like a pikeman in Oliver's New Model Army.

Unless you are a member of the Rothschild family, you are also well advised to have quite a substantial toolkit and at least **some** rudimentary mechanical skills to sort out the various and diverse technical issues and tasks to be dealt with as a part of living in a floating motorised home. The novice or mechanical numpty is also well advised to get membership of RCR - River & Canal Rescue, a sort of RAC/AA/Greenflag of the canals and rivers. Slightly more expensive than the road going equivalent, but then again *anything* even *remotely* associated with boats is priced at a premium.

So by the time we had paid for all that lot, plus the survey & BSS, dry dock, hull blacking and assorted jobs jobbed, insurance and CaRT licence fee, we had forked out well over £2000. Not cheap this boating lark. As people say, BOAT is an acronym for Bring Out Another Thousand.

Next day we needed more smokeless for the fire - but the wharf was a hundred yards or so behind us and across the road bridge. Sighing at our lack of foresight I set off to walk down there and trudge back with a 25Kg sack of coal on my shoulders - when, as I got there, I spotted an old working boat approaching the bridge - selling coal. I stood at the bridge and asked them if they could drop a couple of bags off for us - he said "sure, hop on and tell us which is your boat" so I jumped aboard and arrived back to a shocked and surprised and delighted Lesley as our inner child again showed up on our inanely grinning faces.   Coal Delivered By Canal Boat. Who would have thought it.

And so far we had cruised a grand total of around 200 yards. So time to get to know Hekla in action.

The next morning, bright and early at the crack of 11:00 we untied Hekla and set off on our 3rd, slightly longer voyage. The rolling farmland around Norbury village immediately gave way to the delightfully named Grub Street Cutting.   Dear old Thomas Telford did not mess about with following contours like his predecessor James Brindely - no. he went straight at it. Cutting deep ravines through hillsides, and using the spoil to build tall embankments across the valleys and low ground beyond. (Well, he didn't *personally* dig and build, he did have a small army of Navvies to do the pick and spade work for him, he just pointed at the places he wanted them to dig and build and let them get on with it.)

Grub Street Cutting belies its humble sounding name though. It is a deep tree and fern lined ravine with roads carried across it on tall impressive bridges - the first you encounter it a bobby-dazzler of an affair. The narrow towering stone arch well over 40 feet, with a secondary arch about half way up, with unaccountably, the top of a telegraph pole mounted on it. It must be one of the most photographed bridges on the system.

It was a bright sunny but cold January day, and we were thoroughly entranced by the view and the sedate pace of our passage along the canal. Our three dogs, Max the Mad Springer, his missus Tilly the Mad Field Cocker, and his son Benson (usually referred to as Bloody Benson.) were lying down on the small back deck watching the world glide by….. until Max popped his head up, and took a flying leap into the canal.

26

Now Max was getting on a bit - he was born in January 2000 and was 14 years old - but only physically. Mentally he was still a puppy. And Springer Spaniels and Water are inseparable. We had often walked along the Chesterfield Canal near where we had lived, and his favourite pastime was to jump in and swim to the far bank (where we could not get to him and drag him out) and run/swim along doing what comes naturally - flushing birds from the vegetation.

The off side bank at Grub Street looked far too inviting an opportunity for him to pass up, so off he swam to the far bank - only to discover it did not have a shallow margin for him to ruin along, so he turned back and swam to the towpath to climb out - except that the towpath bank was a good two foot high, so no chance of climbing that, especially at his age. So he turned towards us on Hekla - us having frantically hit the brakes (reverse gear) and come to a stop mid stream.

He swam up to us, I stood on the gunnel holding on to the roof bar and reached down to grab his harness - but it was about six inches below my reach. Not being inclined to let go my iron grip on the roof bar, I told Lesley to steer the boat to the bank, and I leapt off - straight into a good 10 inches of thick gloopy mud. Max, being the clever sod that he is, swam to me, but muggings here had to kneel down in said 10 inches of thick gloopy mud to reach down and hoik him out.

So that sealed the dogs fate from then on. The back doors remained firmly closed when we were on the move. We did try putting leads on and tying them to the roof rails so they could not reach the side, but that put *us* in danger of falling in because they kept tangling us up in them.

That pleasant interlude behind us, we continued on our merry sedate way up the canal, passing several more impressive tall narrow bridge arches then emerging into sunlight onto Shebdon Embankment (where the spoil from the cutting was used.) Half way along Grub Street was a spectacle though. On the off side there is what looks like a small shanty-town settlement with a motley assortment of old boats in various states of disrepair, and a structure holding itself up with what looks like a wing and a prayer, with assorted rusting bits of machinery and oxy-acetylene bottles, and a fabulous old car -

looks like an old Bristol or a Bentley convertible of around 1940's vintage, and a series one Land Rover slowly being smothered in grass and weeds a little further along. We later learned it is a sort-of-boat-yard where people go to get welding and other odd-jobs done from time to time.

We then passed a quaint old pub, The Anchor Inn at High Offley, run by a lovely old lady Olive who has lived there for as long as people can remember - a true old fashioned inn, with wooden settles and church pews by a usually lit open coal fire. It is only in recent years that Olive has bowed to the 20th century and had a beer pump installed on the bar - previously all the beer was carried up from the cellars in jugs. If you are ever passing it is well worth a visit - only opens evenings during the week and lunchtime and evenings at weekends in the summer months.

There then follows a long line of boats on a private off-side mooring, a scene quite common on the Shroppie, where riparian land owners (farmers) rent out moorings. Beyond that is a long straight wide stretch leading to a delightful old canal side wharf at Knighton - it used to be a Cadbury Chocolate factory, and the canal was used to transport chocolate crumb and sugar to and from Bourneville. Now the factory produces powdered milk products, but the old wharf with its roof overhanging the canal is used as a base for a couple or 3 old restored working boats, among them being Birmingham, owned by a social media friend of ours, so again the inner child came out as we shouted to each other "Look. It's Birmingham. Alison's boat." and the cameras clicked away.
Shortly after this we reached our destination for our marathon 5 mile trip at a winding (pronounced winding, and not winding[4]) hole just past Park Heath Bridge. (all the canal bridges have numbers and names - it accounts for boater's odd fascination with bridges, they are the landmarks used to work out just where you are on the system) where we intended to turn Hekla around and retrace our steps back to Norbury. This was our 'shakedown' cruise to make sure we weren't in for any nasty surprises in the middle of nowhere, and to familiarise ourselves with Hekla's handling.

As mentioned previously, if there are onlookers whenever you attempt a manoeuvre or transit a lock, you are absolutely guaranteed to cock up. By the same rule if there is no one in sight, you execute quite tricky and complex tasks with consummate ease. - usually. In this case our turning around did not *quite* go according to the text book, but there was no one around to cause us embarrassment as we rammed the bow and stern alternately into the canal sides.

So we retraced our route back to the starting point, but this time we eschewed the towpath mooring to the north of the junction, which was a 48hr restricted spot, and tied up just past the junction on a stretch with a 5 day time limit on it, where we stayed to further settle in to our new life, with the delightfully quant old country town of Newport just five miles down the road. Also the service block at Norbury was just outside, and these are, in our opinion, the nicest services on the system, so hot showers were in order every day.

It was here that we discovered the wonderful swap-shop culture of the canals. Norbury has one of the best of them, it has to be said, but most service points have at the very least, a selection of books to choose from. At Norbury there are 2 tables, one is covered in books, the other in assorted LQT, MQT and TQT. While we were there people had left a full boxed LPG Patio heater, and a full child's drum kit. We picked up a very nice set of brass electric wall lamps - which as of even date are still sitting in a drawer on Hekla awaiting a supply of TUITS to get fitted. There was a microwave in Hekla's galley, taking up valuable space and we never (or very rarely) use one, so we took it in there and left it for another boater to find a use for.

One of the things that attracted us to Hekla was the separate bunk bedroom, not only because it provides a bed for visitors, but also I would be working from the boat and Lesley had her art, and we needed separate spaces to work in and not get on each others nerves. The bunk room had been a double bunk, but the top bunk had been removed - we could still see the marks where it had been, so we decided to re-instate the top bunk, mainly as a desk/work space for me, but also it could be cleared and an inflatable mattress used to make up a 4th spare bed should both our son's choose to visit for any time.

So I got out my tape measure and measured up - and again and again, then toddled off to the Wharf to ask if they had anything suitable. Simon said that deck-board would be best for the job, he checked and they had a piece that could be cut to my sizes and we agreed a price. I asked the carpenter to come and double check my measurements, which to my astonishment were perfectly accurate. The piece would be cut to size and ready the next day.

I met the chippy in his workshop and we carried this 7ft by 2ft 6 inch solid black board down the towpath to Hekla - in through the front doors and down to the bunk room, which had a 2ft 6 inch x 6ft 10 inch door flanked to the right by a wardrobe filling that side, and a built in vanity unit to the left (that was going to be my desk originally, but proved impractical) - guess what? Despite 15 minutes of To Me, To You, To Me, To You we came to the reluctant conclusion that no way would this quart of wood fit through this pint pot of a doorway.

Still, rising to the challenge, chippy and I had a ponder, and a measure, and another ponder, and came up with a solution of sorts. We would have to cut the board into two pieces - fortunately the wardrobe side of the space still had the remnants of the support for the previous top bunk which would provide a good base for it, so off we trooped with our oversized plank to the workshop and carefully sawed it into 5ft and a 2ft pieces and trooped back to Hekla with some bits of 1 inch square wood to use as supports. Once these were carefully screwed in place the two pieces were reassembled and I had a desk.

Another lesson learned. If you are measuring up for anything on a 6ft 10 inch wide narrowboat - furniture, cupboards, washing machine - don't just measure the space it is going into, but also the bloody doors it has to fit through as well.

All in all I suppose we spent 2 weeks or so settling into our new life using Norbury as our base, but it would soon be time to set off on our life of Continuous Cruising in earnest, and find out what the wide scary world of the canals and rivers had to show us.

<hr>

[1] Say it out loud. [2]
[2] Oh all right. No Fixed Abode. [3]

(3) It is the name of a narrowboat we have seen several times on the Shroppie

(4) Despite what anyone may tell you to the contrary, it is winding as in winding a clock up, and not winding as in wind blowing.

We're Off. - Well, Sort Of Off.

Plan A:
Neither of us are retired, as such. Lesley had her Art degree but the experience ("We know you can draw and paint, you are not here to do any of that, you are here to learn to think and be creative.") meant that she had not produced anything remotely commercial for a while, although she had at last started to work in her favourite medium, pen, ink and watercolours, but she was working at Sherwood Forest in the restaurant - and obviously that job was out of the question when we moved onto Hekla.

I have a small software company producing business database systems. Sods law was invoked when we moved on to Hekla. The 6 months leading up to that Xmas had been exceedingly quiet - but as soon as we made the move all hell broke loose, and I would be a busy little programmer and needed to visit customer sites quite often.

So, Plan A: - most of my customers were around the East Midlands & South Yorkshire area, which is, fortuitously, well served by the inland navigations network, so Plan A was to move over there and base ourselves on those waterways, specifically the Trent, Fosse & Witham, Chesterfield and South Yorkshire canals & rivers Aire & Calder.

But to get there was a bit of a problem, since between November and March each year there are "Winter Stoppages" - works carried on out of the main boating season, lock and bridge repairs which would close the affected sections of canals for anything from a week to a couple of months. In the case of Plan A various closures meant that we could not get to or past Nottingham until mid March that year. Had it not been the case, the trip from Norbury to the Chesterfield Canal at its junction off the tidal river Trent at West Stockwith would have been around 150 miles and 50 locks, and would have taken around 2 weeks at the leisurely pace of the canals.

We had time to kill with Plan A, so we set off from Norbury in completely the wrong direction, North instead of South. We thought we might as well see as much of the system as we could while we waited for the closures to, well, un-close, as it were. So a trip to Chester and back was deemed a reasonable choice - if any nasty surprises of a mechanical or electrical nature arose, then we would at least be back at Norbury to have things put to rights. From there we would be going South again into Birmingham via the Black Country Living Museum at Dudley, then on to Braunston (both places the scene of Art Exhibitions Lesley had attended as a member of the Guild of Waterways Artists but we had travelled by car) and from Braunston, down the Grand Union a bit to Norton Junction then up the Leicester Arm, onto the river Soar eventually reaching Nottingham with time to spare, having taken our time to explore the towns, cities and countryside around that route.

And so it was that on the 7th of February we breezed into the centre of Chester, 20 days after we had moved on to Hekla. The trip had been a wonderful experience for us - despite the seasonal weather, which had included sunny days, rainy days, snow and hail storms, winds and calm, and mud, lots and lots of mud.

We retraced our previous short 5 mile shake-down cruise to the winding hole, but this time we went on into unknown territory. (Well, unknown from the perspective of the canal. Being both brought up in the North West, the Cheshire countryside was frequently visited on day trips) We had passed through Grub Street again, and across Shebdon Bank and eventually into Woodseaves Cutting - a place if anything more dramatic and beautiful than Grub Street - with the added advantage that the name was not quite so mundane and fitted the reality to perfection. Overhanging trees, bare sandstone cliffs, the remains of the ferns from the previous summer, and a long very narrow section where we could have been cruising down the Great Green Greasy Limpopo River - all it would have taken would have been an Elephant trumpeting from the green heights above us, and perhaps a lion or 3 prowling through the verdant slopes alongside the towpath. What we got instead was equally amazing - our first sight of the iridescent blue-green flash of a Kingfisher darting along the canal. This has to be the most beautiful, colourful and dramatic of our native avian species, and every time we saw one subsequently they engender the same excitement and wonder as that first sighting that day in Woodseaves.

A far cry from our first ever sighting of a 'Kingfisher', on our first ever canal boat holiday from Chester to Trevor Basin on the Llangollen Canal. Neither of us have many clear recollections of that holiday, just edited highlights, having been born and raised in the heart of the Industrial North West, within sight of the Dark Satanic Mills of Leigh, and within smelling distance of the sulphur-dioxide odours from Stinky Brook into which British Sidac and Leathers Chemicals occasionally leaked sulphuric acid which coursed through St Helens, so Country Folk we were certainly not - but one such edited highlight was cruising through a leafy section of the Shroppie with the offside bank quite wild and jagged, and the most stately of birds standing in a shady pool at the side of the canal - Which we exclaimed to be a Kingfisher. - a Kingfisher about 2ft tall, slender and graceful, grey and white, with long legs like a Stork and a long pointed beak. Just like a Heron, in fact.

Soon we encountered our first lock at Tyrely Wharf - a very pretty setting with the old canal side building transformed into picture-postcard country houses, with the bonus of a water tap and sanitary station - all be it of the 'bottom of the back yard' style in stark contrast with the glamorous surroundings.

Tyrely Lock is the first of a flight of five locks in astonishingly pretty surroundings, each one only a 100 yards or so beyond it predecessor, and each lock in a prettier setting than the last, culminating in the bottom lock which takes the canal down into another tree lined cutting with sandstone cliffs either side, sculpted by the weather into fabulous shapes - it is like descending into a fairy grotto. An impression reinforced a little further on by a tree stump on the off side which some local has dressed up with a top hat, large smiley eyes, a pipe in its mouth and a fishing rod.

Below the locks and the narrow cutting the canal emerges once again onto an embankment which leads to the edge of the town of Market Drayton. This was our first nights mooring away from Norbury, and we had decided that we would prefer to moor on the off side of the canal if possible so that the 3 dogs could wander and explore without us having to keep an eye open for other dog walkers and cyclists. (Benson had a bad experience as a pup when a cyclist had kicked him and deliberately run over him, so he and cyclists did not mix very amicably.) The offside just here looked attractive - grass and low bushes and trees, so we headed for the side - only to encounter the dreaded 'Shroppie Shelf'[1] . We persisted, and managed to get Hekla tied to mooring pins we hammered into the ground, at a jaunty angle with the bows as close as we could get, and her bum sticking out into the canal a few feet - but we were OK with that, it was late in the day, nearly dark, and there was very little other boat movements at this time of year.

[1] The 'Shroppie Shelf' is a stone or concrete ledge at the edge of the canal for a greater part of its length. Between about 12 and 18 inches wide and usually about a foot below the surface it means that mooring at other than designated places or where the bank has eroded and been replaced with Armco pilings can be a bit, erm, problematic. I have tried to find out why it is

there, but the only answer I get is that "In the old days of working boats they were never expected to moor up along the towpath anyway" - which may be true, but does not really explain this perversely awkward bit of engineering design.

The next morning we untied and learned our first lesson from our mistake. The stretch of water between 2 locks is called the Pound (No, I don't know why either) and these can be as short as a few feet, or several miles. In this case the pound was about 4 miles to the next locks at Adderly. Canal levels are by and large quite stable, but they can raise and fall by a few inches as locks are operated at either end of the pound, either allowing more water in from above, or draining water down. In this case the level had dropped only by an inch or so, but that we sufficient to leave Hekla's 20 tons firmly aground on the shelf.

Much forward and reversing, jumping up and down, jumping from side to side, pushing with the barge pole against the bank, and after about half an hour of these comedic antics we managed to get Hekla free of the grasp of the land and afloat on an even keel once more - and we moved on the sort distance to the designated moorings a 1/4 mile or so along on the towpath side.

The car was left behind at Norbury, so a walk into town for supplies was in order, and rucksack on my back we set off to explore the delights of down town Market Drayton - a place I had briefly driven through one time in the 1970's, and had a favourable impression of. The walk into town confirmed this impression with pretty houses and cottage lining the roads, but the centre itself was a bit underwhelming. The recession had obviously taken its toll, and there was a general air of decrepitude about the buildings and shops.

What should have been a pretty Shropshire market town - and don't get me wrong, it is such - our opinion improved on later visits - but and abundance of charity shops, peeling and flaking paintwork, many closed and shuttered buildings, and a monstrosity of a concrete and steel affair of chain-stores just off the high street left us feeling a little jaded with the whole thing. Plus no sign of a supermarket. We had walked into town along a country lane below the small viaduct at the South of the moorings, and had passed only houses before the centre, but we spotted someone with the black-with-green-piping uniform of a well known supermarket chain, and asking directions we found the small store - one of those bought up and converted on the demise of Netto.

So shopping shopped, the rucksack filled to bursting with what felt like several hundredweight of assorted groceries and alcohol, we staggered back to Hekla by the shorter and less up-and-down-dale route and unpacked our haul.

So underwhelmed were we with Market Drayton that we decided to untie and continue on our way - next stop being at Audlem - another spot where the Guild of Waterway Artists have an annual art exhibition at the canal side mill shop there - and so leading us to our second lesson learned from our mistakes.

It was around 2:00 p.m. when we set off - 'it's only 6 miles' - quickly coming to the 5 locks at Adderly. Not as pretty as Tyrely locks, but nice and rural and enhanced by the farm shop stall in the little shed on wheels by the second lock - although on a Wednesday afternoon in January/February there was not much produce on offer - one remaining box of half a dozen eggs. Adderley locks dispatched, we quickly found ourselves approaching the first of the Audlem flight of locks through another delightfully secluded wooded cutting.

Pulling over to the lock landing, I jumped off and filled the empty lock so we could begin our descent down the 15 lock flight, descending a total of 91 feet over one and a quarter miles.

The Audlem locks are now considered by us as a doddle - each lock only drops by about 6 or 7 feet, they are narrow locks, so the lock gates are not much more than a ton weight balanced well. The bottom gates on a narrow lock are only small - the lock is only about 7ft wide, so it is possible to step-jump from one closed gate to the opposite open gate to save walking all the way around the lock each time. (Health and Safety freaks will be horrified at this practice, by the way, and it is it strictly verboten for any CaRT employee to do so.)

More astute and boaty type readers may have already spotted the mistake leading to lesson #2.

Speed on the canals is general stated in lock-miles, an average being 3 lock-miles per hour. So it takes 1 hour to travel 3 miles on the level pound, and up to 20 minutes to work a lock (if the lock is 'set against you' on arrival, e.g. you are descending and the lock is empty, so you have to fill the lock, open the top gate, get the boat in, close the top gate, empty the lock, open the bottom gates, get the boat out, then close the bottom gates behind you.) so you would, for example, travel 2 miles and one lock in one hour.

Remember we left Market Drayton at around 2:00 p.m. On a late January afternoon. To cover about 26 lock-miles. It gets dark on such a day well before 5:00 p.m.

Fortunately there is a pound between lock 11 and lock 12 at Audlem where there are safe moorings to be had, so we only had to do 23 lock miles that afternoon. We are also quicker at working the locks than the estimated 20 minutes - call it 10 minutes, as these locks are quite shallow and hence quick to fill and empty. Never the less, we did the last 4 locks in complete darkness. Aided by Hekla's twin halogen headlamps and my own LED head torch, and so with a sigh of relief we tied up for the night above lock 12 at Audlem.

At least it wasn't raining.

The next morning we ambled down to the Mill - which was, of course closed for winter. So we peered myopically through the windows for a bit, and wandered up into the village for a mooch around - very pretty place, but the highlight is the little DIY-General Store-Newsagent up the hill a bit, the charity shop - one of the best we've found for variety and value. - picked up a pair of waterproof over trousers for £2, and we stocked up on provisions and alcohol from the co op, than back to Hekla and untie and set off once more.

Down the remaining 4 locks - the last one being the home of Pete's Pork and Poultry - a lovely little place by the lock selling local produce, but at the time having hassles from CaRT & the council for planning issues. Sadly Pete became ill and it no longer trades, but I think the locals have taken over the allotment and keep it in good order.

One away from the busy metropolis of Audlem (called Oddlem by the locals, apparently) we pulled over just a few hundred yards along because of the absolutely stunning view over the young River Weaver valley, with rolling hillsides, lakes and trees, and dairy cows making for the archetype English Country Scene - even on a bright but cold late January day. We stopped the night, despite having to hammer in mooring pins and cope with the dreaded Shroppie Shelf again and the foot wide gap to the bank, to walk the dogs along the towpath and simply to drink in that view.

Next day we set off once again in the vague direction of Chester, passing the delightfully named Coole Pilate, with manicured grass, picnic benches and barbeque stands - well prossibly in summer months, but on a damp January day it is probably a green veneer over yet more mud. But wait. The excitement continues just up the canal when we encounter the large brown sign by the bridge pointing us to The Secret Nuclear Bunker. I bet that confused the Ruskies back in the day.

On to the next town on the route. Nantwich, with the canal passing through the outskirts of the town on another high embankment - again we decided on an off-side mooring before the canal passes over the Chester road - this time with no shelf to get in the way, instead what looked like a nice green surface turned out to be covered in cut back thorny brambles - the dogs were *not* impressed by this, hopping about from foot to foot and coming up to us to pull the thorns out, but it was too late to go any further, so we stopped the night, saving the delights of down-town Nantwich a mile down the road for another time.

The next day off we set again - once on the move I had pressing work to do for a customer, so I left Lesley on the back deck steering Hekla while I retreated to my tiny office/cubicle and set to tapping out software code on my laptop. I had a call from the customer, and annoyed him slightly when he asked where we were, and I described the view from my office window of the sunlit Cheshire plains rolling by outside - while he was sat in his office looking out over an industrial estate in a wet Doncaster.

So engrossed was I in my work that I missed the passing of Hurleston Junction, the turn off for the Llangollen canal, scene of that first narrowboat holiday back in 1983 - from now on we would be retracing that journey, and one thing I did recognise was the canal junction at Barbridge - a tight 90 degree turn off the Shroppie onto the Midlewich arm, with the signpost pointing to Midlewich and the Trent and Mersey canal. I recall passing that junction back in 1983 and wondering what was down there, vowing to return and explore more of the canal system than our little tourist-trap route up the Llangollen.

There followed a long very straight section with cars and trucks thundering by above our heads on the busy A51 - another one of the few Edited Highlights I recall from that first trip - and so arriving at Bunbury Locks. Our first 'staircase' lock flight where one lock empties straight into the next lock with no pound in between. We had done staircase locks before, notably the ones on the Turnerwood area of the Chesterfield Canal - but they were narrow locks. Once past Nantwich on the Shroppie, all the locks are wide locks, and 2 narrowboats can fit side by side. All you have to do when descending is to make sure the bottom lock is empty, fill the top lock and take the boat in, and empty it into the bottom lock, in turn emptying that to drop the boat down to the level pound below.   Since there were no onlookers everything went text-book perfect.

Immediately below the Bunbury locks is the Chas Harden Boatyard, and opposite an Anglo Welsh hire base - at this time of year all the hire boats are tied up having a lie down and rest for the winter from the abuse from the summer holiday hire boaters. This leaves a very narrow channel, 2 abreast hire boats to the left of us, and another row of assorted boats to the right outside Chas Hardens. We breathed in and thankfully didn't hit anything so got through with a sigh of relief.

Another Edited Highlight from 1983 was just around the corner, in a delightful rural wooded setting above and below Tilstone Lock, with its quaint round stone lock keepers shelter sitting by the canal like a tower from a Rhine castle that had lost its way. The offside bank was indented and pleasantly broken up by trees and small inlets, and this was exactly the place where we spotted our first 2ft tall Kingfisher back in 1983.

Continuing on we arrived above Beeston Locks, where we moored up for the night as 2 of my sisters Elsie and Ann who had been following our progress said they would drive down from St Helens to see us and our new floating home. It was another picture perfect scene, with the impressive black and white Tudor façade of the Wild Boar Hotel to our left, where my niece Louise, Elsie's daughter was married in the impressive setting of the medieval room atop the hotel main building, and we had stayed in rooms there - a wonderful extended family get together, all the more so because my eldest sister Marie had come over from Australia for the occasion with one of her daughters, my cousin Wendy. Happy days - but bitter-sweet, as Elsie's husband Bernard was in the later stages of early-onset Alzheimer's, but he was there, wheelchair bound, with a very very nice lad from the care home looking after him.

It was also another remembered Edited Highlight from 1983 - our first overnight stop from leaving Chester, and we walked up into the village to the pub - I recall black and white tiled floors and an olde worlde saloon bar. They allowed dogs in, so we had our 2 Old English Sheepdogs, Emma and Ben with us.   Sadly that pub has gone the way of so many others, closed, demolished, and a tacky-box executive housing estate in its place. Which meant that there is no pub there at all now.

The next day my sisters Elsie and Ann and brother in law John arrived late morning. We moored above the Beeston locks especially so that they could have a short trip on Hekla and experience working the locks - and also *help* in working the locks - then tied up again below the locks and went in search of food. The pub we went to in 1983 had closed and gone, no where else locally, so we drove to Tarporley and had a pub lunch there - I *think* my sisters enjoyed it, but like all our relatives, they think we are a bit (well totally) insane for doing what we are doing.

Once they had gone we fired up the engine again and cruised a short distance to moor for the night in the middle of nowhere again, but with the fabulous sight of Beeston Castle sitting on its craggy hill top across the fields. Its times like this when it comes home to just you what you are doing. Beeston Castle was a place we drove to for a day trip from home in industrial South Lancashire (Not. And I repeat this, *Not* from Merseyside nor the borough of Wigan, Grtr Manchester) but now we had this fabulous view to feast on right outside our living room window.

So far the weather had been dry, mostly sunny, and cold. Off we set off on the final leg into Chester - and straight into a blizzard. Of course these things happen completely out of nowhere. One moment blue skies, the next hailstones then snow. Resulting in a quick dash by whoever is not steering to get something waterproof - by which time you are usually soaked. Thus we passed through the delightful village of Christleton on the outskirts of Chester, eventually getting to the series of 5 wide locks that would drop us down into the city.

A Bonus! After the 3rd lock there is an Aldi supermarket across the canal - moor up outside the pub and walk over the bridge with rucksack on my back, to stock up on food and cheap plonk. I swear this rucksack gets heavier every time I use it. Then down the romantically named Chemistry lock by the old gasometer preserved and painted bright blue for some reason? And the final lock drops us down to the long straight into the city centre.

People had told us *not* to moor by Iceland or unthinkable evil things will befall us, so we tied up on the long straight lined with old warehouses mostly converted into high-end apartments, bars and restaurants, but we were not that impressed by the fact that a road ran directly alongside with no fencing. We would be very nervous about letting the dogs off, so we walked down to the dreaded Iceland supermarket - with a roof top Chinese Restaurant over it. To find a nice quiet place, some mooring rings, a new block of retirement apartments on the off side, and Chester City Walls towering above us - so throwing caution to the wind we walked back to Hekla and moved down under the bridge to tie up in this dark and dreadful spot. Quite apt that Hekla is named after an active Icelandic volcano moored right outside Iceland, don't you think?

The towpath after the bridge led to some steps up to the walls, the slope below the walls was semi-wild with trees, bushes and grass, and the towpath was at that time closed off by temporary fencing so it was not possible to continue to walk along the deep sandstone cutting, according to the notice due to concerns of the stability of the rock face and stabilisation works being undertaken - so it was not at that time a through route for walker or cyclist.

As we moored up there were a couple of young lads fishing in the canal just in front of us - looking for all the world like a couple of typical scouse 'scallies' and Lesley admitted she was a little nervous, so I ambled along to them and got chatting. Cutting through the broad scouse accent, I learned that they hade come down from Ellesmere Port for a bit of fishing, a pair of thoroughly nice lads, it turned out - as usual. People today can be a bit paranoid around teenagers, but generally if you talk to them and treat them with a bit of respect, they generally turn out normal human beings, not young monsters liable to smash your face in with a rock and steal all your worldly possessions on a whim.

We actually found it to be a nice quiet and peaceful spot, with the added bonus that we could let the dogs off for a bit of exercise on the wooded and grassy slopes. We could also step off the boat and within a minute be up on the city walls right by Chester Cathedral. What other way is there to have this historic city right outside your door, other than paying through the nose for a room at one of the expensive city centre hotels - and this was costing us *nothing*. (Well, apart from the fuel - and the 5-figure sum we paid for the boat....)

We stayed there for 2 days, walking the walls with the dogs, window shopping along The Rows (Medieval two-tier arcades) enjoying the usually sights and drinking in the atmosphere of the city on the dark evenings, the wooden walkways echoing to our footsteps - things the casual day visitor does not usually get the chance to experience. During the day we went shopping - February is the best time to snap up bargains in the outdoor shops, so we kitted ourselves up in discounted warm weatherproof clothing, ski-gloves and balaclavas against the worst the English winter on the canals could throw at us. I treated Lesley to a Sterling Silver Celtic Knot ring from one of the shops on The Rows. Generally we had a fine time in Chester, and determined to return one Xmas to enjoy the sights and atmosphere in the festive season.

It's only a couple of hundred yards.

We untied Hekla from her moorings below Iceland, and rather than reverse back under the bridge to the winding (not winding) hole to retrace our steps, we decided to 'nip down to the service point' to empty the toilet cassettes and fill up with water. The service point was just a couple of hundred yards along from our mooring, just down some locks. We cruised past the fence closing off the towpath and into the deep gloomy cutting beneath the northern walls of Chester - under the Bridge Of Sighs to the top of the locks.

Ah yes. The Locks. Northgate Staircase Locks to be precise. A 3-lock descent into Chester Basin where the services were located. Going down is *fairly* straight forward. There are even illustrated instructions on boards at the top and bottom. The top one says "Make sure the middle and bottom lock are empty, fill the top lock, and empty into the middle lock then into the bottom lock" Easy. The bottom locks were empty, I opened the top lock gate and Lesley brought Hekla into the wide lock chamber. I closed the top gates and opened the sluices to drop into the middle lock, opened the gates and Lesley brought Hekla into the middle chamber - I close the gates and sluices behind her and open the sluices to empty the middle lock into the bottom lock. Bloody Hell. That is one *deep* lock. The top lock gate towers up into the sky above Lesley, and Hekla looks very small down there.

And so into the bottom lock chamber - but what is this? Something is floating in there. A Beer Barrel! Treasure! I drag it over with the boat hook and lift it up onto the front deck. It is a Firkin - albeit a plastic one, with the label from a brewery in Lancashire. Obviously some crew had brought it with them on their booze cruise along the canals, and either it fell overboard, or more likely since it was nearly empty, they just dumped it. Anyway we were dead chuffed with our find and I plonked it on the top of Hekla's bows like a figurehead. Childish? Of course!

After all this excitement we steered Hekla to the service point - past Telford Warehouse - now a pub, and tied up alongside the dry dock at the top of the lock dropping down to the Dee branch and the river beyond. Connected the water hose and set that to filling, and got the full toilet cassette and set off to search for the elsan point - which took a bit of finding. It was cunningly disguised as a bottom-of-the-yard brick privy tucked away in the corner over the lock gates.

Job jobbed, we let the dogs off and had a little wander around the area. A quaint old towpath crossover bridge took us to the other side where a new apartment block was nearing completion with a small marina to enhance the ambiance - but the whole area was still just a dusty noisy building site with modern concrete and glass structures arising from the chaos, in stark contrast to the opposite side with Taylors historic boatyard, the terraced houses and an old 'Tin Tabernacle' chapel converted to a residential bungalow.

A quick discussion as to what to do now. Turn around and head back, or continue up the Shroppie to its terminus at Ellesmere Port and the National Waterways Museum? It was the beginning of February, the museum would be closed, so we decided to leave the delights of Ellesmere Port for another day and turned Hekla around to ascend the staircase locks.

Going back up was another matter altogether. Descending you just take your own lock full of water down with you, but ascending turned out to be bloody hard work. Most locks it is to the advantage to have had another boat come the opposite way - the lock is set for you, but with the treble staircase it is actually a disadvantage, and following another boat up makes it easier. But this was February, not exactly the busy season, and the only boat to have used the locks was ours.

Ascending means you have to make sure the bottom locks is empty, then walk up to the top lock and fill it, empty it into the middle lock, then go back up to the top and refill it again. Lesley brought Hekla into the bottom chamber, and I set to empty the middle chamber into it to raise the level of the bottom and drop the level of the middle so that we can get into the middle chamber. While this was going on a young family arrived and the 2 young lads were fascinated by proceedings, and I go chatting with them and their dad. Not really the best of ideas when you are tackling a quite complicated treble staircase lock for the first time. So obviously I cocked it up. But the trick is to make it look like you intended to do it, to avoid embarrassment all round.

Anyway, Hekla is in the middle lock, so I have to empty the top lock into the middle lock to raise the level again, then once that is done Lesley takes Hekla into the now empty top chamber and I have to trudge up to the top again and refill the top lock chamber, and away we go. So "It's only a couple of hundred yards" to nigh on *Three Bloody Hours*. By the time we got back to our starting point it was getting a bit late to carry on, as we would be either ascending the locks in the dark or having to moor up somewhere along the insalubrious Chester suburbs. Plus it started snowing again. So we returned to Iceland and tied up again for the night, treated ourselves to fish and chips from the chip shop on the street above us and ate our supper looking out at the snow starting to decorate our treasured firkin.

The next day, a Sunday, dawned bright and sunny. All the snow was gone, we let the dogs off for their morning

48

constitutional, untied and set off to retrace our trip back to Norbury - and beyond.

The first four of the five locks ascending out of Chester were dispatched without a hitch. All of them were set for us, probably because we were the only ones daft enough to be boating in the cold February weather so they were as we had left them 3 days previously as we descended. The final lock, Christleton Lock was also empty, but there was a tiny 'WaterBug' just arriving at the top - a tiny 25ft narrowboat with an outboard engine, and an old-ish chap on it. I opened the bottom gate for Lesley and started chatting to the bloke - he said he had only bought it 2 weeks ago and was living on it. I was amazed that someone would intend to live full time on something so small. Then I heard a rather panicky screaming shout from behind me - turning I saw Lesley on Hekla rapidly disappearing in reverse back towards Chester..

So picture the scene. I run down from the lock and I am trotting along the towpath towards Chester, while Lesley is shouting at me "It won't stop. Nothing is happening." I shout back to turn the engine off. Which she does, and Hekla slowly drifts to a stop in mid channel. Lesley grabs the centre line off the roof and throws it to me - several times. Until I finally catch hold and tug Hekla over to the bank and we tie her up to the pilings.

I re-start the engine to try to work out what is wrong and Hekla immediately strains against the mooring ropes in reverse. The morse handle has no effect other than to increase revs. So I turn the engine off again and do what I normally do in such a situation, scratch my head and say to the world at large "what the fuck is gone wrong?"

Obviously something has broken. I raise the rear hatch and peer down into the gloom and work the morse handle and nothing happens down there. I have absolutely no idea what the problem is. So out comes the phone and we dig out the number for River Canal Rescue. This is mid-day on a sunny Sunday - but there is always someone there to answer calls. I explain what is happening and the nice lady on the phone obviously has more of a clue than I do about these things, and reassures me that she will have an engineer with us as soon as possible. So we do the obvious and put the kettle on for a cup of tea.

My new best mate on the little WaterBug has wandered down to see if he could help - but he was as clueless as I was, so I walked back up to the lock with him and helped him work down the lock and waved him on his way with my best wishes and good luck on his new life in his tiny bijou floating home.

This is when we experience to camaraderie of the canals. I have the back doors open and the boards up and on the towpath, peering into the engine room trying to fathom out what could be the problem while we wait for the RCR chap to arrive, when a bloke on a pushbike stops and asks if we have a problem. He then comes onboard and proceeds to get his hands dirty delving into the bowels of the engine room and bilge and fiddling with stuff. He says it looks like the gear cable has snapped. He is a freelance boat engineer himself and lives on a boat moored a mile or so up the canal. He spends the best part of an hour seeing if he can jury rig something, but says we really need a new cable, and he doesn't think he has one on his boat. I thank him very much and tell him we have called RCR and someone should be along later. His reply left me in no doubt as to his opinion on RCR engineers. Which was reassuring. Not.

Around 2:00 p.m. and this bloke saunters down the towpath with a large flat box under his arm - the cavalry have arrived. He has a quick shufty at the situation and says he has brought the wrong size cable - so ambles back up to his van for another one. All he has with him by way of tools is a pair of pliers in his pocket. Fortunately I have quite a comprehensive toolbox - *all the gear and no idea.* Neither it transpired had he. He spends nearly 2 bloody hours trying to dismantle the front of the morse handle. Which resolutely refuses to be dismantled despite every available screw and nut being unscrewed. Eventually a light bulb comes on over his head and he peers around the back of the panel, and with a sigh sets to figuring out the complexities of a morse control from the back, in a confined space - *everything* to do with Hekla's mechanicals I later discover is in a confined and bloody awkward space.

It takes him another half hour to finally get the replacement cable installed, and tells me that our RCR Silver Membership, which *should* include the cost of parts up to £1,000 only comes into effect after one month from joining, so I have to stump up £27.50 for the cable. I thank him for his help and off he toddles - by this time it is around 4:00 p.m. and will be dark very soon, so we resign ourselves to spending the night on the towpath at the bottom of some strangers back garden in a housing estate in the Chester suburbs with the traffic on the bypass thundering by over the bridge a hundred yards in front of us.

The next day we set off once more, ascending that last lock without any histrionics this time, and our trip back to Norbury, went without a hitch, with a couple of overnight stops on the way, we were finally back where we started out from, moored on the towpath North of the junction.

Well, I *say* it went without a hitch…. But…. It was raining heavily, we were soaked and cold, and a friend off a newsgroup happened to live close by Bunbury and said he would love to see us and buy us a pint. We came out of the top of the Bunbury staircase lock in heavy rain, and a long line of boats moored along the towpath. We tied up and walked along the canal past the moored boats - and it was Muddy! There was just about room for us to moor at the far end, but it would be touch and go if we could get in to the bank, and the path was a quagmire in the heavy rain, so we said Sodit! And decided to just moor where we were on the lock landing. Normally a practice severely frowned upon, but in the past week we had seen exactly *one* boat on the move, so we thought, what the hell, Marc would not appreciate us traipsing back down through the mud into his car, there were a couple of CaRT workmen at the depot there and they asked us if we were stopping where we were, and when we said yes the replied "Don't blame you!"

Marc arrived - pitch black so he did not actually get to see Hekla, but he drove us to his local, the Travelers Rest in Alpraham, a proper old fashione pub, owned and run by the same family since 1890 and servingood real ales at decent prices. The three of us increased the clientele by 300% and we had a good hour or so bantering over excellent beer. Back to Hekla and a night's sleep listening to the rain pattering on the roof, the wind picking up and blowing a Hooley, we were ready for the next morning and returning to Norbury.

Except we didn't! (Anyone spotting a pattern emerging here?)

Retracing our route North we passed through Nantwich once more - this time we stopped (on the towpath side) and went shopping. Nantwich is a lovely town - if a little stuck up, with the likes of The Cheshire Cat having a sign on the door proclaiming "No jeans or trainers", and for some odd reason an unfeasibly large number of skin care and nail care shops. Its a pleasant enough walk into town from the canal down Welsh Row with its old houses - a row of brightly painted alms house cottages being particularly pretty, and an odd building on the other side a little further on which looks like a nice enough late 19C house with a half timbered Elizabethan house standing forlornly in a semi-derelict state seeming growing out of the left hand side.

As I say, a pleasant enough walk, if a trifle long into the town centre itself, which has a nice array of independent shops in addition to the standard B&M and Home Bargains (more to our pockets' liking) almost next door to each other, and another unfeasibly large array of Charidee Siops - some of them fitting in with the overall pretentious Middle England atmosphere of the town. The Supermarkets, however, both of them Morrisons and Aldi across the road from it, are at the far side of town, with the result that all the heavy stuff has to be carted back in my large rucksack and some shopping bags the mile or so back across town to the canal - which is notably on a bloody great embankment towering over the rooftops of the tacky-box executive housing estate below it - hence a bloody long and steep flight of steps up from the road below the aquaduct. (Look Mr Spell Checker! I *know* it should be aqu**e**duct, but it carries the water over the road and is a Roman word, and the Latin for Water is Aqua, not Aque - well the Latin is actually aqu**æ**ductus, so I can see where the rest of the English speaking world is making their mistake)

I apologise to any Nantwich denizens reading this - I don't *really* dislike they place, its just that is it a bit too twee for my tastes - and I confess to having a smile when, some while later at a lock on the river Weaver in Northwich the lock keeper was chatting to a local and the local made a comment: *"How much? Them's Nantwich Prices!"* Anyway, all that aside, we loaded the shopping onto Hekla and cast off and continued our journey to find a nice quiet rural more dog-friendly mooring further down the canal - and ended up a foot from the bank again thanks to that bloody Shroppie Shelf.

Ever Onwards! We made short work of the Audlem flight - thankfully all of them in daylight this time and moored in the pretty leafy glade above the top locks, which has become one of our favourite moorings on that canal, and then onwards through the remaining Adderly locks (where CaRT contractors had cut down a leaning pine tree and left boater-sized pieces by the lock which filled the roof nicely) and on through Market Drayton and up the Tyrely Locks.

All the while the wind had been gathering strength, and by the time we got out ot the top lock at Tyrely there was a CaRT man there who told us we could go no further because there was a tree down in Woodseaves Cutting, and another large tree now leaning at a precarious angle near Knighton a little further South - so once again we moored on the lock landing for the night to await news than the offending vegetation had been cleared.

Then a boat appeared from the South! It was getting late in the day by this time so we weren't planning on moving on, but we asked him about the tree down in Woodseaves - he just smiled and said "I've got a chainsaw!" - we asked if we would get through and he said he doubted it, he had just cut through the trunk and pushed his way though, so the two halves were in a broken V shape and we would just wedge against them heading our direction.

Then two more boats arrived from the South - this time full of school kids! All running around the lock with their lifejackets on and a gaggle of Young Adults, presumably in charge, trying to herd them into some semblance of order and set them into teams to work the locks. I asked one of the adults what about the fallen tree and the leaning tree - she simply said they had lifted the warning tape up and gone under the leaning tree and managed to get through the fallen tree that the previous boat had cut.   This struck me as a bit of a cavalier attitude to have taken with 2 narrow boat loads of young kids, but I held my counsel. Of course I would have done exactly the same, but not with a boat load of children!

We were stuck there all of the next day, then the morning of the third day dawned bright and sunny and thankfully gale free, and another boat came up. We asked them about the trees, they said that the leaning tree was still there but the tape had gone (presumably broken by the kids boats) and they managed to squeeze through the gap where the other boater had cut the fallen tree, so we decided to chance it while the weather was more clement, untied Hekla and set off.

When we got there it was a bit of a mess! The medium sized tree had been cut in two and either side of the channel and the banks were covered in a tangle of branches. We slowly approached this mess with Lesley at the tiller and I was on the bows watching out - and we immediately ground to a halt! The two halves of the main trunk were indeed angled towards us so that they wedged against Hekla's bow as we tried to pass through. With much reversing and forwarding and myself wielding the boat pole to lever beat the tree into submission, we eventually scraped and crunched our way through and continued on to the next danger point - and sure enough just before Knighton Bridge there was an impressive Elm tree leaning at a jaunty 45 degrees across the cut - we held our breath as we passed beneath it - and as the more astute reader will gather, we did not get crushed to death as it didn't topple down. We also passed a couple of chaps in fetching Dayglo Orange wandering along the towpath who asked us (in a broad Scouse accent) if we could tell them where the fallen tree was?

The rest of the trip back to Norbury was thankfully less of a drama, in bright sunshine, if a little on the chilly side, and we arrived safe and sound to tie up again at our new temporary home ground.

The next day we took the car into Newport for supplies, returning to Hekla early afternoon, and I went to start the engine to top up the batteries - click - click - click. Flatteries completely blatted. - which was very puzzling and worrying, since we had been running every day, so we should not have had a problem. Also there are 3 distinct battery banks, one battery for the bow thruster, one for purely for starting the engine, and 3 x 110Ah batteries to run the domestic stuff, light, fridge, TV etc. so the engine battery should not have been flat at all.

I walked down to the wharf to ask if they could help with jump leads or something, but they said their engineer had gone out on another breakdown, so we called RCR once again. We would not expect an engineer for at least an hour or so, so I left Lesley on the boat and I drove back into Newport as we had seen a battery booster pack in one of the shops, and I bought it - hoping there would be a charge in it. When I got back the voltmeter did in fact show a full charge, so I attached it to the engine battery and - click - click - click

When we were moving stuff into storage I got chatting to another bloke who was also unloading a van into storage, and when I said we were moving onto a narrowboat, he brought out a small suitcase petrol generator and asked if it would be any use to me. Mine for £25. It was only 600W so I said it was not really up to powering anything, so he dropped the price to £15 and I took it off him. It had no petrol in it, and I had not even tried to start it. Also I had no petrol anyway. But by the boat next to us 2 blokes were chatting and one of them had a green petrol can with him - I asked if I could buy a ½ litre from him, and he said no, but you can have ½ litre. Which he poured into the genny's tank, and blow me if it didn't start 3rd pull on the starter.

Brilliant. But I had no jump leads to connect its 12V supply to the batteries, so I improvised and plugged in the charger, which would have taken hours anyway, but then Mark from RCR arrived. He had his huge industrial-strength booster pack, connected it to the battery and it went click - click - click. A quick check determined it was not a starter solenoid jamming, so Mark connected the booster directly to the starter motor terminals and Whirr-Whirr-Whirr-Brooom. We had a running engine.

Mark Stevenson Wood restored our faith in the RCR engineers after the gear cable fiasco, and he went the extra mile to try to check out what had caused the problem in the first place. Apparently with the engine off and all the isolator switches off there was still *something* drawing power from the engine. He spent some time trying to figure it out, but he had fixed the original non-starting issue, and could not spend any more time as he had another break down to get to, so he advised us to have someone check over the electrics as soon as we could, meantime to make sure the batteries remained charged.

What he *did* find, however. Was the answer to a puzzle that had been puzzling us for a while was that we had a digital display panel marked up with "Battery Volts" and "Alternator Amps" but it did not work. I had had the front off and could see no loose connections. I had the box off the other side of the bulkhead in the airing cupboard off and could find no loose connections, but Mark said "What does this switch do?" - a toggle switch just dangling by its wires behind the instrument panel - so he flicked the switch and Lo. The LED display started displaying. Which was super, fab, ace, and all that, but it turned out to be a bit of a mixed blessing, as from that day on - Yay even unto the present, that display becomes the centre of my universe.

Fortunately we had some good friends moored on our route and Ray was an accomplished boat fettler and said he would take a look for us when we got there - this would be in a couple of weeks though, so I kept a beady eye on that display every waking hour to make sure we would be able to start the engine when we needed to.

We Are Off. (again.)

February the 18th, one month to the day from moving onto Hekla we finally cast off and set course for our destination, the Chesterfield Canal.

As mentioned earlier, we had a good six weeks to kill before we could get past the winter closures, so our route would be a circumspect one, using the time to explore the Midland canals while we had the opportunity. The direct route (as if you can call a meandering canal and river as direct) would be about 150 miles, 51 locks and around 2 weeks, hence our short familiarisation cruise to Chester and back.

The day of departure dawned with typical February English weather - a mix of everything. And we bade our farewells to Norbury and the friends we had made there and we were off for real this time on our circuitous route to the canals and rivers of the East Midlands. From Norbury the next settlement is Gnosall - and our first ever tunnel. How exciting.

Gnosall is a small town which embraces the canal as it passes its Western edge, with the popular Navigation pub and the equally popular Boat Inn, both overlooking the canal, and we had been invited to have a drink with a friend Steph off the motorcycle newsgroup uk.rec.motorcycles who was fascinated by our moving onto the boat, so we tied up by the pub and met up with her and her hubby later that night - and promptly got *very* drunk, on excellent beers and finishing of the evening in the UKRM tradition of several shots of Sambuca.

The next morning we delayed departure until the inevitable hangovers subsided to tolerable levels. This was the busiest section of canal we had encountered so far, with boats moored on both sides, and a very tight and awkward bridge to negotiate first thing. An unfeasibly large proportion of bridges on canals seem to be on awkward bends. Then Cowley Tunnel awaited us. - it's only a very short tunnel, 81 yards long, but it was our first, and it was very pretty at that time with a curtain of creepers dangling down over the portal, with a steep sided sandstone cutting either end - and another boat was just entering the Southern portal. - there were a couple of boats moored on the towpath just outside - seasoned old boaters, who eyed us with a little distain as we dithered and flustered and flapped hands up and down wondering what to do. "There's room for two in there you know." they called to us - but we were not convinced, and continued to dither and fluster and flap hands until the approaching boat emerged and we could pass through our first tunnel ourselves.

Beyond Gnossal the canal passes in typical straight lines with the odd bend through delightful rolling Shropshire farmland, at the wonderfully named High Onn the heavens opened - serious monsoon stuff. And we brought Hekla to a halt with the stern sheltered beneath a picturesque turnover bridge (where the towpath changes sides, so these bridges have curved spiralling ramps up one side and down the other where the horses could cross as the tow rope was undone and the boat drifted through.

Beyond the bridge, when the monsoon finally subsided as suddenly as it had begun, was an off-side linear mooring with a really eclectic mix of boats and elaborate decking and shed-like structures - these little floating settlements add terrific character to the canals.

High Onn is followed, predictably, by Little Onn, then Wheaton Aston, famous for having the cheapest diesel on the canal system (incorrectly, as we later discovered), from a roadside garage above the canal by a bridge with a pontoon down on the canal. We had filled the tank at Norbury before we set off, so cannot comment on the price, and anyway it was Sunday and it was closed.

Wheaton Aston also boats a good service point with water and elsan, and you quickly learn the lesson that you never go past a service point. You never know when the next one pay come along, or if, when it does, it has not been blocked by some numpty dumping nappies or other non-dissolvable items down it. Sadly far too common an occurrence.

It also happened to be a day when Formula One was on the telly. So we tied up on the visitor mooring and then went through another of the odd rigmaroles us boaters have to endure, re-aligning the TV aerial and re-tuning the TV. And on this occasion we discovered a 'feature' whereby if the aerial was not aligned correctly to within a few microns, BBC1 locks the TV up completely and you have to pull the power and re-start it to get any sense out of it. This **only** happens with BBC1 - BBC2 and all the other channels work fine. But Formula 1 was on BBC1 - which was a bit of a bummer. So I had to forgo my fortnightly dose of Murray Walkers subdued excitement. And we ascended the final lock on the Shroppie and continued on to moor for the night at the delightful village of Brewood. (Pronounced Brood and not Brewood)

We passed Industrial Narrowboats - the scene of our penultimate boat viewing before Hekla found us, where a boat that looked perfect on paper turned out to be a dark and dismal wreck - but moored on the canal there was Phylis May - restored from the fire that had gutted the boat made famous in Narrow Dog To Carcassonne, and also across the old Roman Road the A5 at Stretton Aqueduct - I have to say that this lurid yellow structure looks more impressive from the road below than it does from the back deck of a narrowboat.

Learning from your mistakes fit the third:

The next day we have a plan. - yes, another one. It takes a long while for it to sink in that Plans and Narrowboats are ill-met bedfellows (or something like that)

The Plan is simple. We have decided to go through Birmingham, with a small diversion to the Black Country Museum at DudLEY. But once at the bottom of the Shroppie, tiz but a short hop to the bottom of *The Wolverhampton Flight* a mere 21 locks. So the plan was that we go to the bottom at Autherley Junction and moor up for the night ready to tackle this mighty mountain fresh and eager the next morning.

Brewood (pronounced Brood and not Brewood) is a short 5 mile lock free cruise to Autherley Junction, where there *should* be moorings before the ridiculous stop-lock with its 6 inch fall onto the Staffs & Worcester canal - *should* be moorings, were it not February and the entire Anglo Welsh hire fleet taking them all up. The area around the canal did not look particularly inviting anyway, so we thought we might as well go through the little 6" drop stop lock and turn right towards the Wolverhampton turn and surely we would find somewhere to moor - not.

So we duly arrived at the turn we planned to make *the next day* and immediately you encounter the first of the 21 locks of the Wolverhampton flight. Ah well, nothing for it, so off we go - the locks are too close together to bother getting back on the boat, so I walked on to each lock - and another puzzle. The first lock was empty, so I just had to open the bottom gates then fill it once Hekla was inside. As were the next 3 locks. "This should be easy. No other boats around, so all 21 locks should be set for us." Hah. 4th lock and the next 6 were all full. Then 4 after that empty, then the rest were full. *How?*

Lesley had wrapped some sausages in tinfoil and put them in the ash pan in the wood stove, so we had a short break half way up the flight to munch on very welcome sausage & brown sauce sarnies, then continued my toil to the top of the flight, passing a mix of parkland, housing estates of dubious aspect, old industry and beneath a towering railway viaduct. It was at least a sunny if chilly day, and there were a few hardy souls wandering up and down the towpath - one such couple stopped as we were working one of the locks and, breathing in, declared that the smell of wood smoke from our chimney was delightful.

At the top - very nice. A row of lock cottages all dressed up for next years "best kept lock" competition, we assumed, judging by the multitude of plaques from previous years awards on the cottage walls. The area above the lock had plenty of moorings in an open immaculately lawned open space - far too open for 3 energetic field spaniels with the busy city centre traffic thundering by un-fenced from the grass, so we eschewed stopping there, as we gave the next visitor moorings after the main road bridge a miss - perfectly safe, as they consisted of nothing more than a 3ft wide concrete platform, about 3 boat length long, with mooring rings, no access except by boat, but at the bottom of a 20ft concrete wall with the inner city ring road thundering by above.

We pressed on. The canal side grew more and more industrial, with semi-derelict old factories, small industrial units, unsavoury looking characters walking the towpath, cans of cider or special brew in hand, we pressed on - for a bit, until passing a large scrap yard on our right the was a large BANG and the engine stopped dead. Into neutral and it started up no problem, but as soon as drive was engaged - clunk. Engine stop.

We were drifting mid channel with no power. I lifted the hatch in the rear deck and for the first time I unscrewed the clamp holding the weed hatch in place and with some trepidation put my hand down into the murky icy water.

To make a short story long for the benefit of non-boating readers, a little bit of an explanation as to what a weed hatch actually is. At the back under the deck is a metal box like structure sticking up, with a metal lid held down with a steel bar and a big hefty T-handled bolt holding it tight. Once removed this box is directly above the propeller, and the rim is about a foot above the waterline. The purpose of this contraption is to provide access to the propeller should anything get entangled around the prop - weeds, for example, bit of rope, sometimes perhaps a lost fisherman's keep net - or in this case a whole king sized bloody duvet cover. Which had caught in the prop and wound itself up into a solid wet 6 inch diameter solid bar of compressed fabric.

Talk to any narrowboater about weed hatch interfaces and you will hear a bewildering and fascinating litany of woes about weird and plain odd things collected down there. Carpets are favourite, as are lengths of electrical cable - shopping trolleys? Entire mattresses are declared the worst - especially sprung mattresses with their inner rusty steel coils snaking all around the prop and shaft. Discarded clothing is common - one boater told me of fishing a silk sari out of the weed hatch in Burnley - then 10 minutes later a second one - and a third shortly after. Some sort of obscure erotic Hindu ritual? Who knows? There seems to be a hotly contested competition for who can collect the most obscure or bizarre object around the prop. One of the best I heard was a whole car tyre, which had somehow managed the clever trick of getting itself in one piece around the propeller - the entire propeller was encased in an un-damaged tyre - which the boater could not slip off as it was such a snug fit. How does this happen?   These and other mysteries are the canal dwellers version of the Marie Celeste and Bermuda Triangle of our sea-faring brethren.

Eventually after about 15 or 20 minutes of hacking and sawing and freezing my arms up to the elbows in decidedly unappealing canal water I release the prop from its new bedding - which sits on the back deck to be photographed. Always photograph your weed hatch hauls - to later be used in evidence to corroborate extravagant claims - and we are off once more - into the gathering dusk.

Our surroundings look extremely dubious, so we resolve to carry on, hopefully to reach the sanctuary of the moorings outside the Black Country Museum at DudLEY. It gets dark. We are in unknown but almost certainly hostile territory. We pass houses and buildings aglow with lights reflecting off the black ribbon of water in front and behind us. The head torch shows us our way in the Nicholson's guide open on the hatch roof, and we finally pass the locks to our left descending onto the BCN Main Line and come to the turn into the DudLEY tunnel arm and our hopefully safe and peaceful mooring for the night. Except that the turn is a tight ninety degree right hander into a very narrow old lock chamber - BANG. We fetch the left hand edge of the coping a resounding THWACK with the bows. But we bounce off (Hekla thankfully has a very strong hull designed to withstand the rigours of hire boat novices) and edge our way to tie up past the last boat on the moorings, our stern by the towpath, the bow rope tied to a ring in the wall of the bridge ramp. It is 7:00 p.m. on a dark February evening.

And Breath and Relax.

We decide to stay put for a day to recover from the exertions of the Wolverhampton flight and the weed hatch episode. The Museum is closed so we can not go inside - not that we probably would anyway, it costing £35 for the two of us, and we know that at the next biannual historic boat gathering the GWA will be exhibiting again and we get free access.

The next place on our route is the centre of Birmingham around Gas St Basin. We have two choices, the BCN New Line which is a left turn and then right and down three locks and a dead straight-ish line into Brum, or a right turn and along the more interesting looking Wolverhampton Level, with its twists and turns and three locks down at the end. We chose the Wolverhampton level - far more interesting, in more ways than one, as we found out later that day.

Learning from your mistakes No.4 in an increasingly lengthy lesson:

The Wolverhampton level looks on the map at least to be a more interesting route. The Main Line drops 20 feet down three locks at its beginning, our route is therefore 20 feet above it, and we keep catching glimpses of it to our left. Two arms leave the mainline at 90 degrees, with the Netherton Tunnel branch passing below us, and the Gower branch turning to our left down the same 20 feet through 3 locks, then we go around a wide loop and cross over the mainline at Stewart Aqueduct, passing 3 locks to our left ascending those 20 feet from the mainline to join us, and finally we come to Smethwick Locks which drop us down those 20 feet to rejoin the main line - well, *should* drop us down those 20 feet, but are, in actual fact, closed for winter maintenance.

So we pull over, let the dogs off for a nose around, while we dither and dally and flap arms around. I walk down to the locks to see how long they will be closed, but as I approach by the state of the works it is obviously not going to be any time soon. Fortunately there is a winding (not winding) hole just before the locks, so with a resigned sigh we turn Hekla around and re-trace our steps as far as the Spon Lane locks which drop us down those 20 feet to the main line, and a *very* awkward 180 degree 30-point turn to head into the city centre. As some wag on social media remarked - "I was laughing aloud at the image

63

I had of you two doing a Keystone Cops back and forwards" - thanks for that.

Lesson learned - we log on to the CaRT web sight and download the list of closures for future reference.

We reach the city as dusk is turning into a wet night and tie up on the main line just before the iconic canal roundabout at Brindley Place, below some posh city-centre apartments towering above us, a building site across from us, and orange street lights illuminating the rain glistening on the towpath pavement.

There are no other boats around, we are all alone in the centre of an unknown city - scary stuff.

We tied up and went for an explore - dogs on leads, which with 3 field spaniels is always an exercise in tugging and yanking on arms and shoulders. It was a wet Wednesday evening in February, not, you would think, the best of times to see Gas St Basin at its best, but the illuminations from the pubs and cafes along the arm glistening on the wet cobbles made for a surprisingly picturesque scene in the centre of Britain's second city, in an area that was semi derelict only a couple of decades ago.

The contrast between the quiet rural settings of January and February were stark - made even more so by an incident the following evening.   We decided to stay for a day to explore the area on foot and have a meal out for a change. Even on a mid week the city was buzzing with life, and the noise and hustle and bustle was almost overwhelming to our eyes and ears more accustomed to the peace and quiet of the countryside for the past few weeks. Back at the boat after an average curry, I was on the towpath with the dogs when a local passing by stopped and gave me a sob-story about having run out of petrol, left his phone at home, needing to call someone to bring him some petrol, or better still get a taxi home to get his brother to come to him - could I lend him a fiver, he would be back within ½ hour and repay me. Brazen or what? I must have been in a soft mood that night, so I handed him a quid or so in loose change for the phone box and said that was all the cash I had on me. He did not look impressed, and we spent the rest of the night listening out for any sort of retaliation attack - thankfully we had an uneventful night.

The next morning we decided to cast off and continue on our way, taking the obligatory photo's of Brindley Place as we went. Our next challenge was the Farmers Bridge lock flight - we were on the summit of the Birminhgham plateau, all the locks so far from way back in Chester had been  rising up-hill, now we were descening. As we pulled over just before the first lock a chap from a nearby moored boat strolled over and asked if we needed any help - then made our day for us when he said "I was going to ask if you needed any help, but I can see you know what your doing."   Chuffed or what?

 Then a CaRT workman just by the lock said he would walk down and set all the locks in our favour for us - what a nice place Birminham is in the day time - In contrast to the attempted scam the night before.

Birmingham and the BCN was turning out to be a city of contrasts - as we descended the locks we were passing underneeth the towering city buildings, with even a posh looking Thai restaurant with picture window wall overlooking the locks, a fascinating place. True to his word the CaRT man had set all the locks and opened the top gates for us and we made realtively short and easy work of the 13 gloomy but fascinating locks.

We then made a left turn onto the Birminham and Fazely canal, descending yet another 8 locks of the Aston flight to bring us out at Salford Junction right besides Spaghetti Junction and following *under* the M6 motorway. The next 3 miles were hardly what you would call pretty, with industry  and decay either side of the canal, lots and lots of rubbish of all descriptions litering the banks and the canal itself. At one point we actually passed *under* a factory. And yet despite these sourroundings I think we saw more wildlife on that 3 mile stretch than we had the previous 100+ miles of rural idyl. Herons, a Fox, more Kingfishers than anywhere else before - or since.

By this time the light was fading fast. At Minworth toplock I had to drag out a huge sheet of plywood and a large plastic drum pallet divider before I could even think of opening the lock gate - all the while watched by 3 local 'urchins' who were chattering away at me in their broad Brummie accents - I can honestly say I probably understood about half of what they were saying, but they were interested in the boat and friendly with it, but we did not fancy mooring up there for the night, so we pressed on down the next lock, reaching the lock landing for the third Minworth lock in pitch dark, and said "Sod It" once again, and tied up for the night on the lock landing, as it looked to be a considerably more genteel area than the previous few miles of industrial and urban decay.

The next morning we had a look below the locks and there looked to be some decent moorings along the stretch just below the last lock, outside a pub with a sign on the towpath declaring that Thursday night was Curry Night. Curry and a beer for £5 - so we thought we would have some of that, and a day off after the multitude of locks we had worked the previous day out of Birminham. Also we spotted on google maps that there was an Asda supermarket a couple of hundred yards away, so we could re-stock on food and alcohol while we were there.

So off we toddled to do our shopping - and found ourselves in the biggest supermarket on the planet. (well, we thought so.) It was *Ginormous*. - we wandered around like a pair of country yokels marveling at this strange world like a cathedral to the consumer. The ethnic food section delayed us for *ages* and we stocked up on a wealth of herbs and spices and curry blends we had not encountered before. Our little shopping trip turned into a marathon session, and before we knew it we were starving and retired to the huge café for some food and drink to keep us going. Eventually we dragged ourselves to the checkout and hauled our booty back to Hekla.

That evening we had a wander around to the pub to sample their Curry Night. We thought. The place was OK, but practically empty, there was no one at the bar, a couple of customers sat around wtching football on the huge TV, one of whom turned out to be the landlord, as he stood up when we asked about the curry - "Sorry, it's not on yet - we only do it in the summer" What? why put the board out on the towpath if you don't actually *do* what you are offering? Well, I didn't actually *say* that to him, we gave him a stern thinking too instead, left and returned to Hekla to cook our own and ate it with some cheap plonk and grumbled to ourselves about it. Well, we are English, after all.

The next morning we untied and set off once more down the Birmingham and Fazely canal, and as we got to the next lock I had to fish various detritus out from in front of the lock gate - but this time it was a pallet. Pallets are highly prized by live-aboard boaters as they make excellent kindling for the fire. In this case though I put it on the roof and it had no central bar so it sat perfectly on the curved roof - so we decided to spare it from its fiery fate and use it to stack other fire wood on.

Lo and behold, at the next lock I fished out a long 6" wide plank - which I measured up and worked out that cuting it up into 4 equal pieces it would make excellent sides to our new much prized wood box. Bonus.

We carried on through our second tunnel of the trip at Curdworth, another epic at a whole 57 yards. Descending 8 of the 11 locks in the next flight we moored up for the night outside the delighfully named Dog and Doublet pub, right by the canal and in pleasant rural surroundings, marred a little by the M42 motorway a few hundred yards away, but it was not intrusive. According to the information we now had, there was a closure at lock 11 which was due to finish the next day, so we settled down and went to the pub after our meal for a beer - and what a delightful pub it is. A proper old fashioned country pub, plenty of local customers (we were the only boat moored outside) and excellent real ales at non-London prices. We found a nice inglenook corner seat and enjoyed an hour or so there before we returned to Hekla for the night.

The next morning we took the dogs for a walk down the locks to the country park, passing the closed lock 11 we were surprised to find CaRT workers still busy. A quick chat and we were told that because of the wet weather the re-opening would be delayed by at least a couple of days to allow the cement to dry properly. Ah well, there are worse places to be stuck for a couple of days than right outside a good pub. We would just have to suffer.

Off to Coventry - ish.

Finally the last lock was open to us, and we dropped down the last 3 locks, exiting lock 11 while the CaRT blokes were still packing their stuff away in their truck - and promptly ground to a halt. Another foray into the weed hatch - but we were adrift in mid channel and a small plastic cruiser was in serious danger of being crushed. But we managed to get to the side - there were a lot of reeds and no solid bank to speak of - and tie to a fence post.

By this time I had learned my lesson about dangling my arms up to my elbows in icy cold and suspect canal water and I had bought a snazzy pair of elbow-length rubber gauntlets from a DIY shop, so armed against the murky depths I un clamped the weed hatch lid and felt around for whatever delights had cause the problem this time - which turned out to be about a dozen plastic carrier bags, shredded by the propeller and tied in a Gordian Knot around the prop shaft. I hacked away with a Stanley knife and pulled out yards of multicoloured plastic, took the obligatory daguerreotype of my haul for later publication on social media, and we continued on our merry way.

We stopped off at the marina just before Fazely Junction and filled up with diesel, then turned left in the wrong direction at the junction to use the facilities and the CaRT services at Peel's Wharf - and what a disgrace. There is a very swish brand new CaRT regional office there, all new brick and green painted metal and shiny windows, with a nice looking little marina at the side - marked No Mooring. A water point, and the sorriest excuse for an Elsan point we had encountered so far. Little more than a low brick wall around a stainless steel sink hole with a lid secured by a padlock opened with the Watermate key, a tap to flush the cassette and a flush handle. Not even a toilet, let alone any facility for rubbish disposal.

We turned Hekla around to face in the correct direction but tied up for the night as the next 3 miles and 2 locks of the canal wound through Tamworth, plus we wanted to have an explore of the delights of Fazely Junction with the snazzy wall painting of a kingfisher on the side of an old warehouse. We also needed bread & milk.

We walked into down-town Fazely to find the Tesco-Express marked on the map was closed for refurbishment, but we got our bread and milk from a garage. Across the road was a timber yard. Another piece of vital equipment lacking from Hekla's inventory was a gang plank. We had not needed one so far, but as an ex boy scout I think it is always better to be prepared, however not prepared enough to pay the ridiculous price they wanted to charge for one at any of the chandleries we had visited. A quick chat with the bloke in the office and he told us to take our pick from a stack of 6 ft lengths of 12x2 timber outside for a fiver.

We then had to thread our way the tortuous twisting route back to Hekla with said (rather heavy) plank balanced on my shoulder, and I could not help laughing out loud at the images of Eric Sykes and Tommy Cooper in The Plank - it was not far off as comic a caper, I can assure you.

Our brand new gangplank sitting proudly on its brass rack on the roof, we set off once more - destination Pooley Hall, where friends of ours Ray and Penny have a mooring. Ray has a lot of experience in fitting out narrowboats and is a wizard with electrics and had offered to take a look at our boat and its problem with the flatteries going blat. After the welcoming greetings and a drink or three we had a meal on their boat and a convivial evenings banter and catch up. Penny is a member of the Guild of Waterways Artists with Lesley and we met them at the annual guild exhibition at the Braunston Historic Boat Gathering every June, and have become firm friends.

The next day Ray came and delved into the rats-nest of Hekla's electricals armed with tools and meters, and more importantly, a clue as to what he was doing. He quickly sussed out that the fancy 4-way isolator switch in the engine room - which has 4 positions, Off, Engine Only, Domestic Only, and Both was wired so badly that in *which ever* position is was in it had all the batteries connected to themselves all of the time even if the main individual isolator switched were thrown. The simplest solution was to just unwire it and lob it in the skip. Which we did, and have not had a problem with the batteries ever since.

We stayed for 3 days, alternating evening meals and drinks on each others boats. (it was far too chilly to sit out on the picnic bench by the mooring) and had a great time. Ray drove us into Tamworth to get supplies from the supermarket and - most importantly - I had ordered a chain saw on-line and had it delivered to the boat yard where Ray often did some work, and we collected it from there, and also a gallon of unleaded petrol, 2 stroke oil and chainsaw oil for my new toy.

The chain saw came in bits, and needed assembling. I had no idea about chainsaws and their workings, only that we needed one to make the cutting up of wombled wood much easier than using a bow saw and axe. With typical Ikea-esque clarity, the assembly instructions were baffling, to say the least.
Eventually I had it all together apart from the main handle and brake which I spent ages trying to fit until I accidentally pulled the brake handle and it slid gently into place as it should. To try to explain, a chainsaw is a two-handed device, one handle on the main body over the motor, the other cross-ways in front just before the chain blade itself. This handle is in 2 parts, the front being the emergency brake, which is spring loaded and pulling it releases a flat steel coil spring which clamps onto the main chain drive wheel and stops it dead in an emergency - like cutting your own foot off, for example. I had spent nearly an hour trying to puzzle out why the armed brake device would not fit over the drive wheel.

Anyway, job jobbed and I had a chainsaw. All I needed was some logs to attack with it. The next day we made our farewells to Penny and Ray - who we would meet up with in June at Braunston, - all being well - which it wasn't but that's a story for another time, so you, dear reader, will see that this book has a bit of everything - romance, thrills, humour and suspense.

We set off the next morning with the flight of locks ascending to Atherstone in front of us. A pleasant enough cruise, and the locks were not too heavy or difficult, especially since there were a couple of volunteer lock keepers setting them for us - until the penultimate lock, when Lesley said she had no power and there was an awful banging noise coming from below.

It was a *serious* noise, and I opened the rear deck hatch to see that the prop-shaft was rattling around in a most un-prop shaft manner. We were stuck in the short pound below the final lock in the flight, and the volunteer lock keepers were adamant that we could not stay there.   So we limped very gingerly into the final lock and out at the top I bow-hauled Hekla the sort distance to the visitor moorings.

Upon closer inspection there was a serious problem with the prop shaft coupling to the gearbox. I phoned RCR once more, but this was gone 4:00 p.m. and we were going nowhere, so I told them not to send anyone that night, tomorrow morning would be fine. I phoned various people, including Ray for any advice, and everyone seemed to think from my description of the symptoms (hardly any drive and lots of serous banging noises from the gearbox) that it sounded like a gearbox problem - which was going to be ouchy expensive.

I decide to get my hands dirty and removed the engine boards for better access to things and took a closer look. I quickly sussed out that the coupling attaching the prop shaft to the gear box should have had 4 bolts, and there was, in fact, only *one* which was half undone. I fished in the bilge below it with my magnet-onna-stick and managed to retrieve another 2, one of which was decidedly bent. I never, even to this day, found any signs of the fourth bolt.

Standing on the towpath having a smoke and a think, I spotted a garage across the wall from us - nothing ventured. So I ambled up onto the road and found my way into the place, which turned out to be an old-school proper repair place, specialising in land rovers and the like, with the owner, old bloke in greasy overalls and wild grey hair and beard, wiping his hands on an oily rag and asked what I wanted?   I handed him one of the bolts, roughly explained the problem and asked if he might have something I could use. He wandered over to a work bench and up-ended a steel box full of assorted old nuts and bolts, sorted through and handed me 6 pre-loved 10mm x 25mm hex head bolts (I did not even know how many I would need, but six sounded a nice round number.   - how much mistah? "just give us the price of a pint." Our Saviour.

Armed with my new fastenings I delved into the engine room once more. The engine room is being a bit generous to describe the rather cramped and awkward place where the mechanicals of Hekla reside, and involved me lying flat across the top of the (still rather hot) engine, my feet sticking through the doorway into the bedroom, my head dangling down into the rear bilge compartment where the prop shaft lived. It turned out to be a relatively simple job to do - just re-align the coupling with the plate at the back of the gearbox and screw the four bolts in as tight as I could - not the easiest of jobs tightening bolts onto something that keeps spinning around itself while you lie on top of a hot engine hanging your head down a dark hole.

Anyway, I was satisfied with my job, and actually felt rather chuffed with myself for sorting a breakdown by myself for the first time. I called RCR and cancelled their call out, and we decided to wander into down town Atherstone and find a chip shop for our celebratory supper.

Atherstone was a delight. One of many old fashioned English small market towns we were set to discover, with lots of interesting independent shops mostly along its main high street - of course all closed at that time in the evening, but we decided to come back again in the morning for a proper browse around - especially the charity shops and in the little handy-man's shop where all manner of tools and bits and bobs were beckoning.

After our morning jaunt into Atherstone we set off once more and our journey took us through the final three locks and onto many miles of lock-free canal. From Atherstone the canal wends its way though Nuneaton - not the prettiest of places on a dull March day, past Marston Junction where the Ashby canal branches off - a detour for another day, skirting to the East of Bedworth, and finally arriving at the iconic Hawkesbury Junction.

The Coventry Canal which we were on passes this junction which is a tight 90 degree left turn under an ornate cast iron footbridge into a small basin with a picturesque pub and cottages and then doubles back another 90- degrees to a stop-lock - about 6 inches of drop - and we are onto the North Oxford Canal.

And….. what a dump. We had been looking forward to this, but the first few miles are crossing a wasteland filled with electricity pylons and wire fencing. Not the best start to what we were looking forward to as a nice rural rambling canal. Eventually we left the doom and gloom behind and were out in open countryside but with the M6 motorway roaring by a few yards away, under the M69 motorway past Ansty village, until eventually we found a nice quiet spot on the towpath in the middle of nowhere to tie up for the night. Then the first large train rumbled by a couple of hundred yards away. Then another 10 minutes later, then another, and so on- all night. Every time a train passed the TV went blank with its [NO SIGNAL] message, then came back on when the train had passed - mostly long lumbering goods trains. I had no idea that there was so much freight traffic on the railways these days. So far the idyllic North Oxford canal was not living up to our expectations one bit. Oh - and it was also *very* muddy.

The next day, however, dawned with clear skies and warm-ish sunshine, as we cast off and continued our journey the canal revealed its better side, and we enjoyed the journey through pleasant countryside, ascending the pretty Hillmorton locks and eventually reaching our destination for that night at Braunston, where we found moorings just past the marina entrance and settled down for the night.

The next day our friends Andrew and Tess from Bedford arrived to visit us and see for themselves our new home. They were not impressed. - Well they liked it, but said that there was no way they could imagine even spending a holiday on one, never mind living in one permanently. Oh well, narrowboats are definitely not everyone's cup of tea. We wandered up into Braunston village and had a pleasant meal and a pint or 2 in the pub. After a wander around the historic Braunston marina and boatyard they said their goodbyes and left us to our new home.

The next day, equally fine and sunny, our daughter Vicky and her partner Anthony and his young son Zac came to visit. Zac was absolutely fascinated by Hekla - and kept us busy as he was running around switching lights on as we trailed him switching them off again. Vicky was using my car, so I 'borrowed' my car and drove into Daventry to stock up on food & alcohol before we treated them to a short cruise up the canal to Braunston Tunnel.

It is exactly 1 mile to the tunnel entrance, but ascending 6 double locks. All the locks since the stretch of the Shroppie north of Nantwich had been single locks, and as we approached the first another boat had just gone in. They saw us coming, and promptly closed the gates and opened the paddles to fill the lock. This is puzzling behaviour and not a little bit Bloody Annoying. They did exactly the same at the rest of the locks up the flight. Not only is it just plain bloody rude, but wastes an awful lot of water, makes it much harder to work the locks, and with only one boat in a double lock chamber, the turbulence causes the single boat to bounce around in the lock - having 2 boats in means that the pair do not get pushed from side to side, so if they were worried about us scratching their shiny paintwork, they were a bit….. well, very thick really.

At the third lock another boat had just come out and the lady off that boat doing the locks walked down and commented to us about them - apparently they looked like they did not have much of a clue what they were doing, she said. Oh well, there is no point in getting frazzled by the idiocy of others, so we continued on our own up the rest of the flight.

Lesley and Vicky were on Hekla with Zac having a whale of a time, while Anthony and I worked the locks. Then Zac found the horn button. It brought a chap out from a pretty lock side cottage to see what all the noise was about. He was Not Amused. Oh well, we are entering The South where people do tend to get a bit uppity.

We tied up at the top on the short pound before the tunnel - by this time it was getting late, and the car was a mile back down the canal - but Vicky had a bad back. So muggings had to unfold his folding bicycle and pedal back down to Braunston to collect the car. My Ged it was hard work. I thought is should be bloody easy because it was all down hill, but I was in 1st gear and pedalling furiously all the way as if I was actually *climbing* a bloody mountain. I got to the narrow staircase footbridge over the exit from the marina and had to dismount - that was when I discovered that in unfolding the bike I had twisted the rear brake cable the wrong side of the handlebar and I had, in fact, been pedalling the whole way with the bloody brake on. There are some thick people about, aren't there?

Anyway, Car returned to the top lock of the flight, Vicky, Anthony and Zak dispatched home (not without some relief.) Tour the boat to find all the lights Zac had left switched on, and settle down for the night before we tackled our biggest tunnel yet.

Early start (for us) the next morning and we ventured into the dark and mysterious gloomy depths of all 2042 bendy yards of Braunston Tunnel.   You would think it would be just dark, but essentially dry in there - but *it bloody well rains*. And because it is so dark, you cannot actually see the water pouring down - mostly from the ventilation shafts - until you get that icy trickle down the back of your neck.

I personally *hate* tunnels. I am not claustrophobic in the ordinary sense of the word, I can be quite comfortable in a confined space, but if I can see a spot of light - in the distance, a light which looks like I will not fit through it, I can feel the tension and anxiety start to rise. As a kid one of the 'games' we used to play was Pile Up, where one unsuspecting lad (quite often me.) was the fall-guy and all the class mates piled on, leaving me buried under 20-odd bodies. If I could see a small glimpse of open sky the sensation of panic was so strong that a sort of berserker rage filled my and I could lift these 20-odd kids up in the air to escape my prison. So it is with tunnels. Braunston tunnel, being as straight as a dog's back leg, was *slightly* better because I could not see the small spec of sunlight in the distance, but I still do not like them, and the panic starts to make itself felt when we eventually see the for portal in the middle distance - but I survived and conquered my demons that day.

Emerging into the weak March sunlight was a relief - and there before us was the boat that we had followed up the lock flight who refused to share the locks. And Captain Slow was at the tiller. For various reasons to do with prop size and pitch, hull profile, and minimum engine revs, Hekla simply will not go as slowly as some boats - presumably with small props and engines tuned for economy above all, so we have a problem following these dawdlers - and I usually manage to peacefully pass them on a decently wide and long stretch - but this chap was **not** happy at being passed - he gave us a glare then pointedly stared straight ahead not acknowledging our presence at all. I had to speed up a little to pass safely - and then I got a right bollocking from a woman walking her dog on the towpath telling me I am destroying the banks.

The thing is that one of the reasons Hekla won't go as slowly as some other boats is hull profile, and she creates very little wash even at normal 3mph cruising speeds, so I was happy we weren't the environmental hooligans we were being accused of. Sod'em.

Heading in the Right Direction

We reach Norton Junction, where the Leicester arm of the Grand Union canal branches off, and we turned left here, finally heading North again. Soon we pass under Watling Street, the A5, and we are alongside the M1 motorway right by Watfrod Gap Services - Truly we are entering The North here. And we arrive at the foot of Watford Locks. 6 locks rising a total of 52ft 6 inches, 2 single locks and a triple staircase locks, and a sign at the first lock admonishing the boater not to even think about going ahead without contacting the lock keeper first.

And where is the lock keeper? Right at the bloody top. That's where. So you have to slog up the steep slope to find him/her to get permission and instructions on ascending the locks. In summer this can be a nightmare, because you can only cross 2 boats in the small pound between the 2nd lock and the bottom of the staircase lock, and sorting gaggles of summer boaters out through this lot is akin to herding cats.

Fortunately this was early March, still in the season of winter stoppages, so traffic was light, no one waiting at the top, so after a brief instruction from the lock keeper abut the order to work the paddles (one set painted Red, the other White) which has the jolly mnemonic of "Red before White you're alright, White before Red and you are Dead"

For those of an inquiring technical mind (non-nerds may like to skip this paragraph) the reason for this is that the Watford locks as also the Foxton locks make use of Side Ponds to preserve water. One set of paddles lets water in or out from the side ponds, the other from above the lock itself - or something like that, I am sure some one will be along shortly to correct me.

Anyway, aside from the thundering roar of the M1 motorway a few yards away this is a stunningly pretty setting, and one you would be very unlikely to see or even be aware of other than by canal. You can possibly see the locks from the M1 through the trees, but it is unlikely anyone ever does. Yet another example of seeing England from a completely different perspective.

A mile or so on from Watford locks we encounter our second tunnel of the day, the shorter (1528 yards) Crick tunnel, then out at the other end we are at Crick, which is home of the biggest and best (so the blurb says) annual canal festival/market place in the country. The Crick Show is a must for anyone thinking of buying a narrowboat - we ourselves spent a fascinating wet and muddy day there a couple of years previously. Lots of boat builders have their latest creations on show, and there are stalls and marquees selling all manner of stuff from boat engines to wellington boots, cuddly toys and bacon sarnies.   For the enthusiast there in their own boats and the masochists camping in the field there is live music and beer tents at night.

This time though it was Just Another Marina and we cruised on by on our merry way Northwards until the day headed towards evening and we found ourselves a nice remote mooring on the towpath right opposite what is marked in the maps as "Medieval Village of Downton (site of)" - well the remains must be exceedingly tiny or bloody well hidden, because all we could see was a farmer's field.

The next morning we set off once more, and after 2 miles of sunny pleasant cruising we came to a junction - with the usual cute olde English style finger posts, Left to Leicester, Right to Welford, and back to Norton Junction, so on a whim we turned right and down the short 1.1/2 mile cut to Welford - just because. And a very pretty little stretch it turned out to be, with one lock, and terminating at a small basin in the village of Welford with a CaRT service point where we paused to refill the water tank and empty to toilet cassettes. There was a short stub where a couple of boats were moored up alongside what looked like the village green, a very idyllic setting, but alas no space for us to moor and dally a while, so we turned around and retraced our steps. At the one lock another boat was just rising, and a second waiting at the bottom. I got off Hekla and swing my windlass in a nonchalant manner I strolled to the lock top gate as the boat in the lock was leaving, told them to hop on, and then, watched by the bloke off the second boat, I proceeded to close the lock gate - the lock gate left open so that Lesley could steer Hekla in. I was quite oblivious to what I was doing until the bloke and Lesley both shouted at me. I blame the unseasonal sunshine myself.

Back to the junction and this time straight on and up the GU towards Leicester, and a short while later our third big tunnel, the delightfully named Husbands Bosworth Tunnel - mooring for the night a mile of so beyond it on the towpath in another delightful rural setting as day faded to night. There was no point in pressing on as ahead of us lay the iconic Foxton Locks which would need a bit of time to work.

So we arrived once more at the top of another flight - this one consisting of 2 separate sets of interconnecting staircase locks of 5 locks each. A couple of years earlier we had visited this place bay car. We had bought our son Ross an adventure card for his birthday in January of that year, and he had opted for a track session at nearby Rockingham Raceway, and we had time to spare so we came here, on a nice warm early summers day. It is a fascinating place, not only for the picturesque and unusual lock flight, but also the remains of the 'Inclined Plane' - a project from the late 19th Century whereby a ramp was built with a pair of counterbalanced lock chambers or Casements which were slid up and down the stone ramps aided by a steam engine. The device was commissioned because of the bottleneck caused by the Foxton locks themselves, but it had a short working life and was abandoned as being too complex and costly to run and maintain. What remains have been preserved and a museum opened in the old boiler house.

Anyway - back to the present and Hekla and the locks themselves. Another sign admonishing us to not even think about proceeding without contacting the lock keeper. Well, remember Watford locks where the lock keeper was based at the top? Well we arrived at the top of Foxton locks to descend, and the old lock keepers cottage was at the top - where would you think the lock keeper would be? Correct. Give that man a coconut. At the bloody bottom. Meaning I had to trek down the 75 foot fall to get clearance and once again receive the instruction "Red Before White" etc. etc. and trek back up the 75 feet to undertake the instructions.

There is a short pound between the two sets of staircases where one boat can pass another, so as we descended another boat came up the bottom set and we passed in the middle. Once out at the bottom we were faced with continuing North to Leicester and beyond, or the irresistible temptation to fork to the right and explore the Market Harborough arm.

This involves a right turn - but there is a pedestrian swing bridge immediately on the turn, so you have to swing around to let someone (me) off to go and operate the bridge - which is bloody heavy. Once through that, there is yet another road swing bridge a few hundred yards further along - this one turned out to be jammed. A call to CaRT got me a return call from the local engineer who said. "Not again." and gave me some instruction to try - mostly jumping up and down on things and hitting things as hard as I could, which eventually got the thing working again and we continued on our way to Market Harborough.

This was another very pretty short canal arm of about 5 miles to the basin at the end, passing some absolutely fabulous canal side gardens, but also a very stinky meat reclamation plant producing ingredients for dog food. We turned in the basin at the end as there were no visitor moorings available - all being full of the winter hibernating hire fleet based there, so we tied up on the towpath and walked down into the town for essential supplies.

It is yet another un-written rule, or an old charter, or something, that when you moor up to go shopping it is *always* down hill to the shops, with your light and empty rucksack, hence it is *always* bloody well *up-hill* on the way back with your half a ton of food and alcoholic refreshments on your back. And Market Harborough was no exception. True it is a prettier town than most, but it is still a bloody hard slog back up to the mooring.

Back on the boat and we didn't want to spend the night there, as the towpath was a busy place with walkers and the like, and we were at the bottom of someone's gardens and overlooked by houses, so we moved out of town to moor up at our preferred location, out in the sticks where the dogs could have a bit of freedom without us worrying too much about walkers and cyclists. Another night where I could admire the view from my smoking room overlooking a valley with a main road running along it in the distance, and drink in the view of the twinkling lights from street lamps and houses in the distance from our dark and secluded country retreat.

The next day we set off once more back to Foxton and turned right again to continue our Northern progress - this time I new the knack of the awkward road swing bridge at Foxton village, and on through a pretty secluded section with was sign posted as an SSI (Sight of Special Scientific Interest) which adjured us *not* to attempt to moor up anywhere hereabouts because us nasty boaters may harm the indigenous and specially interesting local flora and fauna.

Onwards and through yet another tunnel, the shorter 800 yards Saddington tunnel, followed by 5 locks reasonably well spaced apart, and at 3 o'clock that sunny afternoon we came to a very pretty spot at Newton Harcourt, where we decided to stop for the night in very amenable surroundings with a country park and open fields for the dogs to romp in over the far side of the canal. The village itself is on the towpath side, and over the bridge is the old quaint manor house and its picturesque Norman church with one grave memorial in the church yard a scale model in stone of the church itself. - very nice.

Onwards. The next day we continued Leicester-bound, and discovered something worse than the supermarkets down-hill empty up-hill loaded - a mile each way walk along a busy dual carriageway in hot sunshine. (In *March* ?) What a drag. Before that we had 12 locks to work, a call into the CaRT services at Kilby Bridge for the usual water, elsan and rubbish disposal, and an amusing run in with an angler who was half asleep and didn't reel in his line - which caught on our prop and resulted in him running down the towpath after us, fishing rod in hand, shouting for us to stop. We relented and did so and he tried to reel in his line - leaving the float broken free - but at least it came off the prop so I wasn't in danger of getting a fish hook in my had down the weed hatch. We finally stopped for the night at Glen Parva by a country park, where the dogs were spoiled once again with a romp in the fields.

The next day we moved off into the Big City. After, that is, we were scared silly by the *huge* weir just before the last of 11 locks that morning. The canal was a mix of urban and rural as it twists and winds along broadly following the course of the river Soar - and at times it actually **is** the river Soar - until you come to Freemans Meadow lock overlooked by Leicester football stadium - and it is a very wide, very high, very strong weir - When I say *we* were scared silly, *I,* of course, was not phased by it one jot. But Lesley was decidedly nervous and I had to make sure that Hekla was securely tied to the lock landing before I worked the lock.

Beyond that we were in another world. Straight as a die, tree lined, ornate bridges, and Hekla competing with a small flotilla of rowing skiffs, canoes, and all manner of rowed craft on the still waters in the city centre. There were plenty of canal-side moorings, but we had been told to make for Castle Gardens as being the best and safest of them. City centre moorings can be a bit, erm, lively of an evening, especially at weekends - and this was the weekend.

The City Gardens mooring turned out to be an absolute delight. It is on a floating pontoon - always a good thing on any river navigation - with a secure fence and locked gate which lead into the municipal gardens - and best of all, the other gates to these gardens were locked 6:00 p.m. with one gate useable for boaters with our magic BW Watermate key - so in effect we had a large ornate and private garden all to ourselves. And the city centre and fascinating market are just a short stroll away.

We were doubly glad to be there later that night when a nearby nightclub opened its doors and hoards of marauding drunken merry-makers descended across the opposite side of the canal, and we saw a couple of youths ride up on a bicycle - presumably stolen, and proceed to chuck it into the water.

We shared the mooring with one other boat with a couple and their 2 late-teens/early twenties daughters, and they were very pleasant and informative, and the next day when we set off they set off a little while later. As we approached Abbey Park I realised that we were adjacent to Leicester's Golden Mile with its wide range of Indian and Pakistani shops, so we moored up and went for a wander - this was a Sunday, but most of the shops were open, and we did a lot of window shopping admiring the highly colourful and exotic goods on display. One thing we did pick up on was that we had our 3 dogs with us and most of the other pedestrians were extremely nervous of the dogs.

We went inside a couple of the Asian grocery shops and stocked up on a wide array of exotic fruit and veg, curry mixes, and even treated ourselves to a selection of Indian sweet-meats. If you have never been to Leicester a stroll down the Golden Mile and a visit to the city market is a must, especially if you like curries as we do - although some of the vegetation on offer requires a little on-line research to work out just what it actually is and what, exactly, to do with it.

Returning to Hekla, unloading our shopping and casting off, the other boat we had shared the Castle Gardens mooring with came along, and in total stark contrast to the ignorant sods back on the Braunston flight they not only insisted on sharing with us, but also said the it is better for both boats to enter the lock side by side, as one before the other can end up with a bit of shuffling about as the first boat usually does not sit quietly to one side. The next four locks were thus dispatched in double-quick time, until we bade farewell to our new best friends at Thurmaston where they were mooring.

The next stretch took us though Watermead County Park, a delightfully picturesque place, especially on a fine sunny day. There were lots and lots of gongoozlers about, and as is my wont, whenever I could I roped them in to help at the locks. At one lock there was a fair crowd watching us from the bridge over the canal, and as Hekla left the lock I closed the gate on my side, and rather than walk around to do the other I shouted for someone to close it for me - with fairly comic results. Here was all 5'6" of me in my Herculean Frame (I had put it on especially) closing my side with an air of nonchalance, when first one, then 2 then 3 big burly blokes struggled like buggery to shut the other one. I thanked them with a cheery wave and left all 3 gasping for breath.

A little later, again we were exiting a lock when a family rolled up on bicycles - I assume they were a family, but they were a very well regimented one, as the Dad stopped and around 5 kids all lined up regimental parade style while 'Dad' gave them the benefit of his wisdom about the workings of locks, when I shouted to hem if he wouldn't mind closing the gate for me, he looked puzzled and said "I don't have a key." (meaning a windlass) - I said "You don't need one, just push this beam." and I trotted down the steps and onto Hekla as the all lined up and *heaved* with all their might - finally closing the gate.

And off we went into the sunset, now on the River Soar proper, (well, actually the River Wreake, but it's more or less the same thing) and we moored for the evening at Sileby Mill, above the lock, and - gasp - across from the weir. It was still quite early and the chandlery at the small boatyard below the lock was still open as we went for a bit of a wander and explore of our new home for the evening. And we encountered our first blatant prejudice from another boater against 'Continuous Cruisers'

We bought an ice cream in the chandlery - well, we bought 2 'Mivvis' - a favourite from both our childhoods - a strawberry flavoured ice lolly with an ice cream centre. And as we unwrapped them outside the shop there was a chap sat on the bench eating his own (a cornetto or something) and we got to chatting, and he asked where we were headed, and we told him, and he asked where our mooring base was, and we said that we were live aboard and we were Continuous Cruisers - to which he sneered - and I *mean* sneered. He said in a voice dripping with scorn: "Huh. Continuous Cruisers. Continuous Moorers more like!" stood up and said not another word but walked off as if we were polluting the air he was breathing. We wandered back up to Hekla and he was on his boat, moored up just behind us. He saw us, gave us a glare, and without a word he started his engine, untied and set off.

We were gob-smacked. It was getting late in the day, there would be nowhere for him to moor for quite a while and I'm pretty sure he would have ended up mooring up *somewhere* in the dark of night. But he was obviously so incensed at the very concept of Continuous Cruisers that he did not see fit to share a mooring space with us in case we contaminated him? (See Appendix a) for a brief rant about the Politics Of The Canals)

We had a peaceful enough night without him anyway, and next morning we descended the lock and tied up alongside the dinky little fuel barge outside the chandlery to fill up the diesel tank, and off up the Soar proper to Barrow On Soar where we tied up by the service point -as there was nowhere else to moor - for a brief look around, when a very shiny boat pulled up and asked if it was OK for them to tie up alongside to fill their water tank. A very pleasant couple, just setting out for their 'summer season' and offered to share the next couple of locks with us, then they were mooring near Pilings Lock Marina to meet up with some friends.

Unlike the previous couple we shared the Leicester locks with, these people eschewed going in together and insisted on one at a time - which was OK, but a bit of a faff, and we definitely prefer going in alongside the other boat if they are amenable, it is much easier.

Leaving our New Best Friends behind we pressed on through Loughborough, where yours truly made a total hash of the 90 degree right hand turn at the junction of the short Loughborough arm, and rammed the far concrete bank with some force. It was just one of those occasions when, for whatever perverse reason, Hekla did not want to obey the tiller and refused to turn - it had happened before, and has happened since, and there seems to be neither rhyme nor reason for it. Bloody perverse, I call it. Hekla often has this unnerving habit of wandering off. If you come up to a likely looking spot on the towpath with pilings to tie up on, come to a smooth halt parallel to the bank and jump off, you had better have the centre line in your hand, because like as not the bloody boat will take it up itself to go and have a look at what the far bank looks like. Perverse is not in it.

Anyway, with Loughborough behind us, (well, *most* of Loughborough, we had a few bits of it on the bows of Hekla after my, <cough> contretemps at the turn) we carried on past Normanton on Soar - apparently a delightful place to visit, had they provided *any* facilities for mooring up there. - and moored for the night at Zouch (Not Ashby De La, just plain Zouch) where we encountered a friend off Facebook who we had never met in person, and had a long chat and catch up. We were by now a little ahead of ourselves after all the dashing from place to place, so we opted to slow down a little and had a Day Off at Zouch to recharge the human's batteries.

After our day off - we were bored. The village is just a single street, although there are some nice walks across the fields and along the river, we set off once more. This stretch of the Soar is one of the prettiest

river sections on the system, winding along and passing pretty villages, posh houses, pubs etc. although the locks, especially Kegworth Deep Lock can be a bit intimidating. At Kegworth Deep we were disappointed that the local semi-tame fox declined to honour is with its presence. Perhaps because we had 3 dogs on board maybe? But apparently this fox is often to be seen sat by the lock playing the part of a 4 legged bushy tailed gongoozler watching boats transit the lock - he/she may also be on the scrounge for snacks from the boaters though, which is probably nearer the truth.

Further on as we approached the confluence of the Soar and Trent we passed Redhill marina and there is a truly wonderful and eclectic variety of boats moored all along that stretch and at the boatyard itself, by the final flood lock. There are boats of all shapes and sizes, both moored on the river and up on blocks on the river side, and alongside the final stretch are some very nice houses seemingly built into the cliffs bordering the river itself. It is a varied scene though, because looming above all this rural idyll is the huge Radcliffe on Soar power station casting its shadow - and at the time we were passing the busy A453 - a road I have spent many unhappy hours queuing on - was being widened and the river side was akin to a building site with mud and clay and portacabins and scaffolding and various and diverse construction site paraphernalia littering our view from the boat.

Once past this we were greeted by the very intimidating sight of the huge weir by Trent Lock - all perfectly safe and the foolish boater protected from being swept over into oblivion by a boom cable with huge cylindrical floats in a fetching shade of Day-Glo orange, but it is still an intimidating sight none the less. Then we were on the Trent proper, in a seeming vast expanse of water, with the Soar behind us, Trent Lock onto the Erewash canal in front of us, a right turn onto the Cranfleet Cut towards Nottingham or left up-stream to the beginning of the Trent and Mersey canal at Shardlow.

Shardlow, being one of those 'Must See' icons of the canals, was chosen as a small diversion from our route and a bit of sight seeing was in order, so off we toddled, approaching Sawley Cut and our first experience of all electric locks. And somewhat confuzzling they are to novices such as us. Never the less the pre-adolescent child in me had sussed out the sequence of button presses to operate the locks with minimal fuss, then we found ourselves on the lock landing, with signs absolutely forbidding us to use the CaRT facilities, which are *supposed* to be accessed from the pontoon back on the river itself - ah well, sod it, we were very daring and took our rubbish over to the skips anyway. The heavens didn't open, no thunderbolt from on high came down to smite is, so I think we got away with our little transgression against the roolz (again)

Along the Sawley cut passing another eclectic mix of boats moored there - although these looked somewhat more up-market than many of those at Redhill, we called into the posh marina for diesel - and another first, a self-service diesel pump. Put your credit card in, and fill up just like many supermarket filling stations. The only drawback being that the red-diesel duty split is fixed at 60/40, making it expensive for a live aboard who uses the diesel primarily for domestic use to heat water and generate electrikery.

And so on, past the very elaborate and expensive wide beam boat moored by the diesel pump wharf, and out through the flood lock back onto the wild Trent. Passing under the M1 motorway was another treat, after the number of time I have driven along it over the years. Amazingly I had seen the wild waters cascading down from the weir, but had never noticed the navigable Trent - something that came home quite frequently in the future as we saw main roads we had driven along countless times blissfully unaware of this Other World of the canal right alongside or underneath us.

Then we came to another crossroads. (cross-rivers?) with the lock raising onto the Trent and Mersey canal dead ahead, the un-navigable Derbyshire Derwent (not to be confused with the navigable Yorkshire Derwent) to the right, and the river Trent continuing to our left for a short navigable distance to Shardlow Marina. We went straight on to the Trent & Mersey lock to fulfil our little bit of Canal Kulture fix at Shardlow.

Which was, to be honest, a bit of a let down. Oh it is pretty enough, with the iconic canal warehouse with its clock tower - but that has been turned into an up-market pub. And a fascinating canal side house with an very extensive sit-on model railway track around its garden - but *no where to moor.* Well, there was, if all the mooring hadn't been occupied or were decidedly un-savoury looking and not exactly dog-friendly, so we turned around at the winding (not winding) hole and retraced our steps to a more rural mooring above the first lock - right opposite a water & sewage treatment plant, where we spent a peaceful if rather aromatic night, and rather masochistically we stayed over another day & night, so that we could explore the delights that Shardlow had to offer and to browse the chandlery there. I did some work, and Lesley did some laundry.

The next day we moved on again retracing our steps back onto the river Trent to Trent Lock, where we turned in to explore the Erewash canal. Earlier in the year a friend had been moored just above the lock when torrential rain and flooding kept them stranded for over 2 weeks, with the lock landing completely underwater. We were hoping not to have this experience ourselves.

The Erewash Adventures

Trent Lock has to rank amongst the prettiest canal settings on the system, in my opinion. The lock is set back from the river so that boats can tie up safely on the lock landing without fear of being swept away in strong flows, and the landing itself is a series of terraces in a curved arc bringing to mind the Roman Senate or an ancient Greek amphitheatre. Overlooking the lock is a quaint olde worlde café, although one of the elaborate signs outside proclaiming "Good Old Fashioned Dripping Toast -   A round of thick cut toast smothered in Farmhouse Dripping" did not exactly set my taste buds a-tingle, but I am sure *someone* might be tempted by it.

Flanking the canal are a pair of pubs, the Trent Lock (a rather snooty up-market affair, posh food, posh prices, and not dog-friendly) and the Steamboat Inn - probably *The* most dog friendly pub we have encountered - on the night we went into the bar for a beer there were more dogs than humans in there. And the beer was good as well, and not too pricey.

Of course we did not dare bring our three thugs in there or it would have prossibly meant a rapid change in pub policy, as our three - Max the Mad Springer, Tilly the Floozy Field Cocker, and their pup (Bloody) Benson the Manic Sprocker regarded all territories as being **their** pack territories and no interlopers were to be tolerated.

Just above the lock is one of the ubiquitous CaRT signs - but this one a little different from the run of the mill "No Mooring", "Water Point Only", "Cyclists Please Dismount" <Ha. As If any would obey *that* one.> - this one reads:

Attention
Dog Owners
Pick up after your
Dogs, Thank You

Attention Dogs
Grrrr, Bark, Woof

Opposite the Steamboat Inn is a working boatyard, dry dock, and a number of old working boats tied up, including one belonging to a Motorcycle Newsgroup friend, fellow boat enthusiast, and part time author of historical canal articles. This was a pleasant surprise, as I knew he had a boat, but this was a very nicely restored working boat and he even sold coal from it.

Just up from the lock on the off side of the Erewash canal is a very eclectic mix of boats and houseboats, ranging from somewhat tatty old narrowboats - one with its bows protruding into a lean-to shed-cum-greenhouse affair built out over the water from a substantial bank-side shed, some truly astonishing 2-storey Floating Bungalows with elaborate railings and top deck patio areas - more reminiscent of a paddle-wheel-less Mississippi River boat than an English houseboat - one even had a huge fairground floating swan pedalo moored up beside it.

Next day we cast off again to explore the nether regions of the Erewash. It is a varied canal passing from the rural Tent Lock and immediately plunging into the urban sprawl of the East of Nottingham. Passing under the railway bridge you are immediately surrounded by the urban scenery of Long Eaton. An awkward S bend under a bridge takes you past a Sea Scouts hut, with a rather amusing and over-sensitive alarm system which Hekla set off with her mere presence and prompted it to warn us through a speaker system to "Stay Away From The Building".
The road over the bridge we had passed under becomes the canals companion for a mile or so, separated only by the pavement, and the childishly amusing sight of a speed camera apparently aimed at the canal - over 30mph on a narrowboat? Gizza Break.

Ever onward. Through Long Eaton and out the other side, through Sandiacre past the headquarters of the rather wordily entitled *Erewash Canal Preservation and Development Association* housed in an attractive old lock cottage, conveniently located at the side of Sandiacre lock. They have a wibble site for more information at:
http://www.erewashcanalpreservationanddevelopmentassoc.or g.uk

The scenery encountered by this under rated and under visited waterway is varied to say the least. Passing the back gardens of terraced houses, and splendid old industrial buildings, some restored and 're-purposed' as offices or apartments, some in a sadly neglected state and crying out for renovation.

We pulled in to moor at one such location in Sandiacre overlooked by impressive old buildings converted to up-market apartments and a grassy area on the opposite bank - and ideal mooring spot were it not for the proximity of a busy main road and its attendant traffic noise. We walked a short distance to the local dAli supermarket for supplies, mooching around some interesting local independent siops as we went, and suitable re-stocked we untied and headed off to find a more rural and dog-friendly spot to moor for the night

We passed under the delightfully named Brian Clough Way (the A52 from Nottingham to Derby) and the M1 motorway roared over our heads a short while later, as evening began to approach and we found a pleasant enough spot to moor between Sandiacre and Ilkeston.

It is an odd thing about being on a canal. You can in some places be right in the middle of a bustling cityscape, and yet down on the cut it feels like you are in the middle of the country. The canals often pass unnoticed through our towns and cities and are a ribbon of green countryside in the midst of concrete, brick and glass. So it was with our 'quiet rural mooring spot' - looking at it on google earth we were in fact sandwiched between and old works spoil heap and a busy railway line, but we could see and were aware of none of this from our cosy towpath location.

The only fly in the ointment was that the towpath the entire length of the Erewash has been 'upgraded' and is grandly entitled "The Erewash Valley Cycle Way' It has to be said that the majority of cyclists on the towpath are quite considerate of others, but there is always the minority of Lycra Louts who treat the towpath as a racetrack. We also discovered a new cycling hobby on the canals around Nottingham, of Night Cycling' with blindingly bright LED head and flashing tail lamps these can come swooshing past the boat at all times of the night. Most odd behaviour if you ask me. One false move, one misplaced fallen branch and they would be in the water. Oh well, each to their own.

The next day we were to be graced by a visit by our 2 sons. Ross and Mike had decided that we were close enough that they could afford the petrol to come and pay their first visit since we moved on to Hekla.

To help them find us we moved up the canal a short way to Ilkeston and moored outside the delightfully named Gallows Inn pub. Of course they didn't find it, and we had a phone call mid morning asking where we were? They had turned up about half a mile further up the canal, and said they would walk down to meet us.

Ross and Mike saw Hekla for the first time (and us for 3 months.) and were very impressed. We untied and took them on a short cruise a mile or so up the cut -and coincidentally through 2 locks, just to give them a full flavour of the life their Mum & Dad were now leading. While they were here we took full advantage of having a car and driver at our disposal and make another excursion to a supermarket. (There **is** a limit the how much wine and beer one person can lug around in a rucksack.) and we settled down to cook us and them a curry. (prossibly their chief motivation in visiting us - two twenty-something lads sharing a house do not a Masterchef make)

We had a very pleasant day with them, they enjoyed the mini-cruise - Ross had a go at the tiller, but Mike demurred. I think he was *still* in denial about us selling our house, to be honest) and a friendly family chat around mouthfuls of Onion Bhaji, Naan bread and Rob's Special Rogan Josh Chicken and King Prawn Curry, and they set off down the pitch black towpath with a borrowed torch back to Mike's car. (As the astute reader with adult offspring may suspect, we never did get that torch back.)

It is lovely when our family visit us - but it is also lovely when they finally leave and we can sit back and relax with a glass or three of wine, perhaps a whisky as a nightcap, in the cosy glow from the fire and a couple of lights in our warm wood-lined cocoon.

93

We spent that night on the edge of Ilkeston and the 3 dogs were getting a little stare crazy, so we moved on the next day just a couple of miles and moored up again below Eastwood Lock, a short distance shy of the terminus at Langley Mill with fields and woods for the dogs to work off their excess energy. (and Field Spaniels have a *lot* of energy to burn up. Even the 'old man' Max, at 14 years old and still going strong.)

While exploring the little nooks and crannies we came across a very nice piece of old dry tree branch lying perfectly supported by the remains of the tree it had presumable come from, so we fired up the chainsaw and sliced it up into stove-sized pieces and relayed it back to Hekla in the Big Yellow Bucket especially saved for the purpose.

Next day we moved off once more and arrived at The Great Northern Basin. A grand title for the present terminus of the Erewash canal, and the place where in better days the basin was the junction of the defunct Nottingham canal and the Cromford canal. Both of these canals, as are a great many across the country, are being supported by local groups and very slowly being restored, although many face a difficult future, especially the Nottingham canal which has had large stretches obliterated as the Nottingham conurbation has expanded and developed over the intervening years since it was closed.

There are visitor mooring here which are signed as 5 days, but longer may be negotiated by contacting the local preservation society rep who has a boat moored there, which we did, and decided to stay for a full week. We also got a form to apply for the plaque available to boaters proclaiming "We Have Navigated The Full Length Of the Erewash Canal" - not many boaters venture up here, which is a shame as it is well worth the effort.

We decided to stay because we were close to 'home' and we arranged for one of the kids to drive over with the car and we drove them back so that we could keep it with us to explore the area and do some serious shopping, since Ikea was just up the road. There is also an Aldi store within a hundred yards or so of the mooring, as well as a large Asda supermarket a half mile or so up the road in the centre of Langley Mill.

We trudged around Ikea on the look out for a table for our main saloon on Hekla. We found what seemed to be the ideal solution in a hardwood folding table - intended for outdoor use, but it was solidly made and both side folded down so it could be stored to one side when not in use.

Back at the boat we manhandled it into the saloon, and sat down at our 2 leather captains chairs to eat lunch - which immediately highlighted a slight flaw in our cunning plan. Sat on the chairs, the table top was at shoulder height. We looked like a pair of TyPhoo Tea Part Chimps sat there reaching up to get at our plates.

Back to Ikea then. And we struck lucky. A folding table sort of thing, but just one leaf, no legs, but a strut at the back with holes in it to screw to the wall. Result. The other folding table found a home on the front deck where it fits nicely and opens out for al-fresco eating when needed - and later as a platform for displaying Art when we got our Floating Traders license - but that is another story for another time.

After a week at the basin we decided it was time to set off again and get into Nottingham in time for the lock closures to finish and we could be on our merry way up the Trent to our intended extended base on the Chesterfield, Foss/Witham, Trent and South Yorks navigations.

At the Langley Mill basin there is a dry dock hired out to boaters at reasonable rates for DIY hull blacking, and while we had been moored up one boat was in there doing just that. As we were about to untie the owner came over to us asking if we were heading back down to Trent Lock, if so we could share the (double) locks with them - which was very brave since his boat was all pristine after the repaint.

We obviously agreed. Doubling up through locks makes life *much* easier, especially as he had his wife and teenage daughter with him to help work the locks, and we set off in tandem. Through the first lock OK, by the second one our new best friend told us his wife and daughter were having a 'bit of a domestic' which resulted in the both storming off swinging windlasses and setting the locks ahead for us. We still had to open & close the top gates and open the paddles to drop the levels, but it made the whole trip a lot faster and easier than doing it solo, so thanks to a little PMT and Teenage Angst we made the 11 miles and fifteen locks in record time. We took 2 days coming up, and just over half a day getting back to Trent Lock.

Thankfully our New Best Friend did not suffer any scrapes or scratches on his pristine newly blacked hull in the process. Much to his relief, because by the looks on the faces of his missus and daughter he may not have survived to reach their home mooring in one piece.

We moored up at Trent Lock that night, and the next morning I caught the train back to Langley Mill to collect the car. We hung around a few days, moving off the Erewash to moor on the floating pontoon on the Trent itself, which gave us very nice views from our windows, and added entertainment as a large group of kids and their minders turned up and pitched tents on the land around the sea scouts place across the river and we watched them having a whale of a time in their dinghies.

Time to move again, the closures on the Trent below Nottingham were due to reopen soon, but first sort the car out. Ross caught the train from Newark - and the jammy sod got it for free. The ticket machine at Newark Castle station was out of order, so he was going to pay on the train, but no one came around checking tickets, the time to catch the connection at Nottingham to get to us was too short to use one there, and there was no one checking tickets on that train either. No wonder these train companies need so much of our taxpayers money in subsidies.

Ross stayed the night with us, and the next day we took him for a cruise to find Diesel for Hekla - there would not be much chance to refuel once we were onto the Trent and the last leg of our journey 'home' to West Stockwith. We crossed the river and headed back down the Soar to Kegworth where there was a boatyard selling the cheapest diesel we had seen so far at 88p/litre but when we got there, late morning, it was closed.

We have since passed there a several of times and have yet to find it open. Which may be a blessing in disguise because the sign said Cash Only and we don't normally carry that much cash around, preferring to use plastic to pay our way.

Since they were closed we turned around and came back up to the Trent and turned Left upstream to Sawley lock and the boatyard & marina on Sawley Cut, where we found the diesel pump there was self-service - just like many supermarket petrol stations - put you card in, fill up, get a receipt. Only the price was 95p/Litre. Which is not much compared to road diesel prices, but when you fill with over 100L it all adds up.

Job jobbed, we took Ross further up the Trent to the Derwent to turn around and retrace our route back to the pontoon at Trent Lock where Ross could take the car back home - and one of boating's little niggles occurred, when we got back to the pontoon it was empty apart from one small plastic day cruiser moored *right in the middle of the pontoon*. Of course this was right next to the ramp up onto the back and the posh Trent Lock pub, so the poor people had a few yards less to walk. But it is generally not the done thing to plonk you boat right in the middle of a mooring and take up so much space that we had to moor with our stern sticking out beyond the pontoon. Sure enough and hour or so later the party of yuppie-types staggered back down from the pub and set off tacking their way upstream towards Sawley lock.

We tugged Hekla back to make a more secure mooring stem and stern on the pontoon, said our goodbyes to Ross and settled down for the night, ready for the leg into Nottingham the next day.

Messing About On The River.

All fuelled up and ready to go. The final leg of our maiden voyage from Norbury to 'home' on the East Midlands & North East waters. We cast off from the pontoon at Trent Lock and onto Cranfleet Cut, through the open flood lock and down the lock at the end and onto the Trent proper for a very pleasant cruise under clear blue skies, with this stretch of the Trent a beautiful twisting delight, passing islands and riverside moorings with a truly eclectic mix of boats and structures, with the odd island thrown in for variety, the Attenborough Nature Reserve on the Northern bank, while the view to the south across farmland to the wooded ridge sets the picture off to perfection.

Until you get to Beeston Lock.

Don't get me wrong. The lock and the approach past moorings and Beeston Marina are as pretty as you like, but to the right of the lock itself is the *huge* and very intimidating Beeston weir, and you feel like you are heading straight for it as you approach the lock entrance, which is angled slightly to the left. This was made much, much worse by the antics of another narrowboat playing silly buggers.

As we were approaching this clown unmoored from the marina pontoon on the left and mover *very* slowly to the lock landing, and then proceeded to turn around. We had nowhere to go. The river flow - not a flood, but quite a strong current never the less, was insistent that Hekla should go and make friends with the float barrage above the weir, and we had to use some power to turn Hekla and head back upstream to relative safety while matey boy took his leisurely time turning his boat around in the safe shelter of the lock approach.

Why he could not wait on his pontoon while we got into the lock will remain one of life's little mysteries. Being charitable you could say he didn't see us until he had committed himself, but the plain fact was that he did see us coming and hurried to untie before we got there, so charity can go back home where it begins, and we will settle for plain old fashioned anger, thank you very much, especially when he compounded his 'crime' by hogging the service point moorings just past the lock, making us tie up on the lock landing opposite to wait, where a powerful by-wash pushes the boat away from the landing. *Then* - after a long wait, he turned his boat around and went down the lock back onto the Trent to moor up where he had started from. He had performed his anti-social manoeuvre simply to get to the servie point before us.

Sometimes it can be very hard living up to the laid-back idyllic dream of life afloat - especially when someone who has, only moments before, deliberately put you into a position where your boat, if not your life, have been put into jeopardy by some puerile self-centred actions. Made worse by the cheery wave he gave us as he passed us heading back upstream. He obviously had no bloody idea of the drama he had, wittingly or unwittingly, caused to unfold by his actions.

Quite often on river navigations your gently meandering around bends is interrupted by a sudden lock, usually with a weir to one side, as the engineers back in the day made the rivers navigable by the simple expedient of making a canal - or a cut - to maintain a navigable depth as the river flows downhill. These cuts tend to be quite short and allow the canal to pass a drop in level of the river. Usually there is a flood-lock at the upstream end, which can be closed in times of, er... flood, with a proper lock at the downstream end lowering the boats down to the new level of the river.

The Beeston lock is slightly different though, as it was built to maintain the canal levels taking it into the heart of Nottingham, joining up with the old Nottingahm canal which used to go all the way up to join the Erewash canal at the Great Northern Basin at Langley Mill (where we had come from a few days previously) The junction of the Beeston Cut and Nottingham Canal is quite distinctive, as the Beeston Cut makes a sharp 90 degree right turn onto all the remains navigable of the Nottingham canal for just under a mile to drop down onto the river Trent once more just below Trent Bridge.

At first it is semi-rural, with housing on the North bank, and a country park between the canal and the river Trent. There is also a good CaRT service block just above the lock with toilets, Elsan disposal and even a shower - but the water tap is stupidly placed at the side of the building a good way up and back from the canal, so the boater needs quite a long hose to reach from it to the boat to fill the water tank.

In about a mile or so the housing gives way to industry, and the Boots factory prominent on the North side, and the scenery turn increasingly more industrial as it progresses into the urban sprawl of central Nottingham. There is Trevithick boat yard along here with a number of interesting boats moored there, including a very posh looking Gentleman's Cruiser - mid 20th C style which would not look out of place in an episode of the Poirot detective series.

Deeper and deeper into the city we finally get to Castle Marina and a long stretch of visitor moorings under the shadow of Nottingham Castle, with a handy Sainsbury's supermarket right by the canal - next to the <spit> HMRC offices.

We still had a few days left to kill before the winter closures finished allowing us to continue on our way, so we lingered in Nottingham and wandered the city centre. In a previous bridge-boat interface (with Lesley at the tiller, I hasten to add (I *know* I will get merry hell over this.)) the TV aerial proved to be not as tough as 18th C brickwork and was a little, erm, bent and distressed, so we found Maplins (eventually.) and bought a natty little black plastic box designed specifically for fitting to vehicles (mobile homes, truck cabs etc) to replace our poor tangle of steal and aluminium.

It was strange mooring right in the city centre, as the towpath was a pedestrian and cyclists highway into the city. People watching is a favourite pastime with me, and it was fascinating to see the mix of characters going past, especially on their way to or home from work. You could tell the affluent young yuppie types, with a spring in their step or often lycra-clad on expensive bicycles, with earphones in and the latest iPhone in a prominent brag pocket and the latest designer rucksacks, handbags or man-bags. These in sharp contrast to the lower echelons of Nottingham workers, often in baggy sagging cheap black suits with scruffy black shoes and a plodding weary gait as the trudged by.

Across from where we moored was a busy main road, but directly opposite us between the off-side bank and road was an old brick building - just a small flat-roofed square utilitarian old work hut with no door on it, but an old discarded arm chair outside the open doorway. Later that night we noticed a glow from inside it, and over the next couple of day we found that is was being used as a shelter for a couple of homeless people. They were quiet and unobtrusive, no nuisance to anyone - but across the road were some pretty posh looking city apartments, and sad to relate that the next time we came this way that building had been completely demolished.

So here we were in Nottingham waiting for the clearance to get on our way up the Trent to West Stockwith. Only 61 miles and 8 locks to go, 2 or 3 days easy, when the CaRT notices email dropped its bombshell in my mailbox. Holme Pierpoint lock, the first Trent lock downstream from Nottingham closed. Apparently the lock gate had jammed, they had no idea why, so divers went down to investigate and discovered that the entire lock chamber had dropped about a foot. Prognosis was not good, and they estimated repairs to take up to *8 weeks*.

The Long Way Around

We did not really fancy sitting in the centre of Nottingham for 8 weeks. Not that we have anything against the place. Well, other than it being a city, noisy at night and some quite hostile natives. We were used to (mostly) spending our days and nights out in the peaceful quiet countryside away from the hustle and bustle of 21st C life. The prospect of spending 8 weeks with a view of the side of a supermarket on one side and a busy main road on the other did not appeal one bit.

But what to do? Well, turn around and find another way, obviously.

We studied the maps and books, and plotted various options on Canalplan.org (a valuable online resource, an almanac of all things canal related, and an excellent route planner) and we decided that the only thing to do would be to retrace our steps to Trent Lock and continue on to the Trent & Mersey canal at Shardlow, up the canal to Bulls Bridge north of Stoke On Trent, onto the Macclesfield canal to Dukinfield, then the Huddersfield Narrow over the Pennines and down the Aire & Calder to the Trent at Keadby and upstream to West Stockwith. Our remaining 61 miles and 8 locks suddenly became 209 miles and another 183 locks.

Before we set off Lesley had one more item she wanted to buy, some enamel paints from the Hobbycraft store in Nottingham. We decided that since we had to turn the boat around anyway, we would sail Hekla to within ½ mile of so of the store to save our legs, so off we went and had a jolly time confusing a fisherman. He was fishing from the towpath just short of the end of the canal, and he had to pull his pole in as we came past.

We were on the lookout for somewhere to moor as close to the shop as we could, but ended up arriving at Meadow Lane lock and the few moorings there were already taken. We (well, I) spotted a likely looking winding (not winding) hole, so we reversed back to it - passing the same fisherman again, who had to pull his pole in again, and I set about turning Hekla around - only I didn't. The winding (not winding) hole was certainly wide enough to turn in - just. But unfortunately the undergrowth and mud on the far side thought otherwise and I managed to get Hekla well and truly wedged across the cut with the bows in firm embrace of a tree on the far side.

Just our luck! The un-written rule about boating is that whenever you cock-up there is guaranteed to be an appreciative audience of gongoozlers on hand to add to the embarrassment. In this case it was a gang of local kids on the main road high above the far bank. They obviously thought it looked good fun, as I was stood on the bow with the proverbial 10 ft barge pole, fighting the embrace of the triffid-like vegetation on the small bank of soil there, and climbed eagerly over the wall and scrambled down the undergrowth to offer advice and assistance.

After much heaving and shoving and cursing from me, and shouts of instructions and abuse from Lesley on the throttle and tiller, I gave up on the idea of turning and we gradually broke Hekla free of the mud and overgrown vegetable embrace - and ended up still facing the wrong way. Nothing for it - we moved forward, passing our new best friend the Fisherman once more, and went down Meadow Lane lock, out onto the wide green greasy Limpopo <sorry, Trent>, turned in a wide arc and re-entered the lock, rose up, and for the *fourth* time passed our new best friend fishing on the towpath. By this time we were almost on first name terms with him.

We had spotted some mooring rings a little further back, so we tied up there and walked back down the towpath - passing our New Best Friend for the *fifth* time to go trek across the city to Hobbycraft for the Lesley's paints. I am sure it would have been less hassle to order the bloody things on line and have one of our kids drive them down to us. And as is often the case with these things, Lesley wanted only to buy some paints, but we came back with the paints *and a sewing machine*.

Shopping shopped, we retraced our steps - past our New Best Friend for the *sixth* time and back to Hekla. After all this kerfuffle time was marching on, darkness would be falling well before we could get back to Trent Lock, so we had no option but to return to the mooring we had left near Castle Marina and spend the night there again before setting off tomorrow on our Long Way Around journey.

The next morning we set off - or not, as the case may be. Engine started, all ropes untied, push off from the bank, engage forward gear and......... nothing. The engine revved OK, but we were going nowhere fast. Well we were going out into the middle of the canal slowly, but neither forward nor reverse gear were working. Cast adrift with no propulsion yards from either bank. I hailed a passing walker and asked for help. I threw him the centre line and he tugged us in to the side and we tied up again. I had no clue what the problem could be. At first I though the bolts on the prop coupling had come adrift again as they had back in Atherstone, but nope, they were all present and correct. Cable broken (again) as it did in back in Chester? Nope, all present and correct. So nothing for it but to phone up good ole River Canal Rescue again.

In less than an hour our saviour strolled down the towpath to sort us out. We told him what happened, showed him what happened, and he smiled in that irritatingly knowing way that these people have, and said he knew what the problem was. A quick delve into the bowels of Hekla's bum end and he checked the gearbox dipstick to find no oil present.

Apparently it is a common fault on our gearbox - a PRM150 - a small 'O' ring fails where the gear change linkage shaft enters the box and it spits all the oil out - the gearbox is hydraulic, therefore no oily no worky.

He toddled off back to his van for a replacement 'O' ring, and while he was gone the weather decided to have a right stroppy tantrum and the heavens opened. I don't mean just heavy rain, I mean monsoon rain. Bouncing off the floor rain. It caught the RCR man out in the open on his way back from his van and he arrived soaked through to the skin. We offered him towels and tea and shelter until the rain subsided, but the plucky man said no, he was already wet through so he carried on working in the deluge - which eventually stopped, and he replaced the errant 'O' ring - it was a *very* fiddly job, to fit a part costing about 5 pence. We also learned something new again - the gearbox takes bog-standard 10-40 engine oil, of which we had some, and once topped up all was working as it should be once more.

We thanked our saviour profusely and once more untied and set off on our Long Way Around trip. Back along the Beeston canal to the Trent at Beeston Lock. Once down the lock and out on the lock landing below I spotted the river level warning markers - green for OK, Yellow for Caution and Red for "Don't Bother." and the water had just gone into the yellow - problem is you can only actually **see** the board once you come out of the lock onto the river. Lesley was very concerned, but I mustered my supply of bravado and said: "We'll be Fine." and off we went upstream.

Hekla *loves* rivers - well she loves deep water, and seems to come alive on the rivers, so we were delighted when we arrived at Cranfleet lock in much the same time it took us to get downstream from there to Beeston - but against what was obviously a very strong flow. By the time we got to the lock landing at Cranfleet it was completely submerged. Fortunately opposite the stone lock landing is a floating pontoon landing, which we tied up at and I worked the lock bring Hekla up onto the safety of the Cranfleet Cut - much to Lesley's relief. The flood was so bad that the flood lock at the other end of the cut had been closed however, so we had to tie up where we could and wait it out.

Next morning and the flood gates were opened, so off we set once more, past Trent Lock and the mouth of the river Soar - the waters were still quite high, and the river was flowing pretty briskly. We came up behind a converted working boat with its vintage engine Chug Chug Chugging along but going nowhere fast. As we passed him we slowed a little and asked if he needed any help, but he said no, he would make it - eventually.

We got to Sawley cut and I jumped off and went up to set the electric lock cycling to empty and allow us to raise up, but we waited a while to make sure the old boat we had passed made it, and kept the lock ready for him so he could just come in and share it with us. As the waters rose he said he had come up the Soar and had wondered what all the red lights meant. The Soar has red warning lights for flood conditions rather than painted boards, and he had come up in flood conditions - fine on the Soar heading *down* stream with the current, but turning left onto the Trent against the current was another matter. Still, he had made it. It turned out later that the chap was the father of a facebook friend, who told us his Dad had mentioned us when he spoke with him a few weeks later.

We offered to accompany him on to Derwent Mouth lock and onto the calmer waters of the Trent & Mersey canal, but he declined, saying that he didn't want to tempt providence again and he would stay the night on Sawley Cut and let his engine have a rest after its exertions fighting the Trent in full flow. Hekla did us proud however, and we rose up onto the beginning of the Trent & Mersey Canal and we pressed on, covering some lock miles, eventually coming upon Mercia Marina, where we had visited a couple of years previously in our boat searching days, so we could not resist turning in an topping up the diesel tank and having a browse around Midland Chandlers - we bought some of their own-label blacking to touch up some of the scrapes on Hekla's hull when we had the chance, and some stern gland packing, since Hekla seemed to be a bit leaky around that area.

We moored for the night a little further along past Willington village, and the next morning continued our journey and stopped at Burton on Trent, mooring at Shobnall Fields, the sight of the IWA rally we drove to a couple of years previously. There was a Lidl supermarket a short walk into the town, so we stocked up on food and cheap plonk while we were there, and the next day carried on our merry way.

Once out of Burton the canal passes Branston Water Park, where we might have moored up and explored, but having Max with us would be a nightmare as he would be in the water at the first opportunity and we didn't think the bird watchers and wardens would appreciate a Springer Spaniel doing what Springers do best and scaring every bird in sight. So we pressed on and the canal soon had the busy A38 as a close noisy companion for the next 3 miles.

At Alrewas, after the short river section where the canal and Trent become one for the last (or first, depending on your direction) time, we were hailed by Bobby who we had met back at Zouch, but the moorings were chocker block, so we could not find anywhere to tie up - which was a pity because Alrewas looked like a nice place to explore. Instead we carried on and rose up the first 2 locks at Fradley Junction - another iconic canal scene and tied up on the visitor moorings there. A pint or two at the Swan was unavoidable.

While we were there Lesley took the opportunity to take some of her art works in to the gallery there where a friend of hers has some of her work on display. She left some prints and cards on 'sale or return'.

Off we went once more, up the remaining 3 locks at Fradley on a fairly dull day, and made it as far as Colwich before the light began to fade and we found a towpath mooring for the night. Our route that day took us through the towns of Armitage and Rugeley, and we took childish delight in passing below the high walls of the Armitage Shanks factory and playing 'spot the bog' in the yards either side of the main building.

Only a short trip the next day because we decided to turn left at Heywood Junction and moor on Tixal Wide. Everyone seems to rave about Tixal Wide. It was the result of the local landowner objecting to the canal passing through his land, so he insisted that it was made a *lot* wider and landscaped as an ornamental lake. There is an impressive folly overlooking the wide, and it is a very pleasant setting and place to moor - other than the fact that the bank is *very* low, only 6 inches or so above the water level, so its a big step down (and up) off (and onto) the boat.

It was here that I decided to risk all and re-pack the stern gland.

For the non-boaters, a bit of a technical aside (boaters may want to glide past this bit, or stay and snigger at my lack of knowledge, please yourselves)

A narrowboat has an engine and a gearbox just like a car (sort of) but instead of driving wheels it turns the prop shaft - about 2" diameter stainless steel shaft with the propeller on the other end. Now more astute readers may realise that this shaft has to go through the hull to the propeller, therefore there is a hole in the back of the boat, and the shaft turns quite quickly so boats have a variety of ways to keep the water on the *outside* of the hull. In Hekla's case there is a Stern Gland, which is a fixed tube going to the outside, and a sleeve arrangement on the inside, like this:

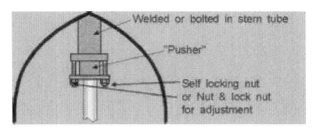

Inside this sleeve there is 'stuffing' - basically some (expensive at about £10/ft) square section rope material that is wrapped around the prop shaft and 'stuffed' into the hole where the sleeve goes. (The 'pusher' in the above drawing)

What you are supposed to do is wrap your stuffing tightly around the shaft like a screw thread, then cut it with a (non)Stanley knife at a diagonal so you end up with three rings of stuffing. You do this *before* attempting the next bit, which is the scary bit.

You unbolt the 'pusher' and pull it forward towards the gearbox - at this point there is not a lot to stop the water gushing in and sinking you other than a bit of grease and the old worn out stuffing material. You then get a sharp pointed stick and try to dig out the old stuff, and which point water starts to come in - fortunately the fixed stern tube is only just bigger than the shaft, so the water only comes in at a steady slow trickle like a kitchen sink tap not quite shut off. You then push each ring of the new stuffing into the gap, with the joints offset against each other, at something like 12 o'clock, 4 o'clock and 8 o'clock. Shove them back in with the Pusher, and carefully re-tighten the bolts evenly so that the pusher is straight and not twisted to one side of one side of the bolts is tighter than the other. And that's it. Job Jobbed.

Its all a bit of an anti-climax, to be honest, because the first time you attempt to DIY this job you are bloody terrified you are going to sink the boat. Not helped by having to do all of this while lying across the engine with your head and shoulders below the stern deck.

Which reminds me. Another boat-techy bit for the non-boater. On top of this stern gland with its stuffing, there is a brass tube with a tap handle on top. From this there is another narrow tube connected from the bottom of the brass tube and into the top of the stern gland. Inside this tube is grease. It is like a grease gun and what you are *supposed* to do, if you remember, after every cruise is to lift the hatch on the stern deck and give the tap a couple or three turns - this forces grease down the thin tube to aid lubrication and water-tightness of the stern gland.

You can - and usually do forget to do this *every* time. I try to have a routine whereby every time we moor up I remove the tiller arm and then grease the stern tube. At the end of a run the frequency of water drips from the stern gland has usually increased, so forcing more grease down should slow this down - if not stop it altogether until the next time you move the boat.

The water (well actually its greasy water) drips into the bilge in the stern. This is separated from the engine bilge which is a steel box around the engine area, so that any oil leaks from the engine do not get into the stern bilge and get pumped out into the canal by the bilge pump. It is still a bit environmentally worrying when you see the oily film when you pump out the bilge, but there really is not a lot that can be done about it, other than to have a bottle of dilute washing up liquid to hand to squirt onto the mini oil slick to dissipate it.

The next day, having had our thrilling experience mooring on Tixal Wide we spun Hekla around - easy to do in this wide lake-ish stretch, back to Great Heywood Junction and turned left to continue our Northern course for home.

Just up from the junction is Great Heywood Marina, where we had called in to look at Badger, mentioned back up there ^ somewhere - so we pulled in and tied up to the jetty by the office and bought a gallon of Morris's best 10w40 engine oil - the re-stuffing of the stern gland must have awoken a spirit of DIY fervour and I determined to change the engine oil. Car maintenance usually involves and oil change at a prescribed interval of so many thousand miles or once a year, for example, but boats to not have odometers, the engine is run not only for propulsion but also when moored up to charge the batteries and heat the water, so instead of an odometer we have an Hours Run meter.

Early on I started keeping a daily log recording engine hours run that day, mooring location, notes on the day and any events or expenditure like filling with diesel. Initially I only made a note when we filled with diesel - we had no idea how much the tank held so we were a bit paranoid about running out of diesel - no fuel gauge either, you see. So it was 41 days into our life afloat before I started to fill in the log every day. This is a long winded way of explaining why we did an oil change, since we had now done 420 engine hours since we took over Hekla (we had a full service with oil & filters at that time.) I had no idea how frequently the oil should be changed, but various "experts" on t'interweb suggested anything from 200 to 500 hours. Our friend said he only changed the oil when he felt like it - usually once a year. But his engine burned and leaked oil so frequent top ups kept the oil reasonably fresh - well its one way of excusing it.
We left the marina - first having chatted to the brokerage boat about Badger, which was till moored there and up for sale, and cruised on to find a decent rural towpath mooring, which we found just past Weston on Trent.

It was a pleasant sport, and we spied a very distinctive building across the fields - a sort of Tudor Mansion style affair which was a ver' ver' posh 'otel and restaurant. We had passed this every day for a week and more ferrying stuff to and from Hekla when we were moving on. It's a little thing, but we found it fascinating and amusing.

We stayed there for 2 days while I did the engine oil change, Lesley did some laundry and we generally spent some effort in cleaning the boat and housekeeping which we had been neglecting in our enthusiasm for our new nomadic life.

Oh yes - the Laundry. Have I told you about the washing machine? No? Well now is as good a time as any I suppose. It was a bit of a contentious issue, this washing machine. Lesley had set her mind on a small automatic washer, which would fit nicely in the 'utility room' (a.k.a. ex-toilet). Conversations on't interweb lead us in the direction of a certain very small automatic machine which looked like it would fit in the space available from the dimensions given on the web sites, there was a water supply I could tap into, the 240V ring main was nearby - the only awkward bit was the waste pipe, but at worse we could drain it into the shower next door and let the gulper[36] pump it outside.

We were on the verge of ordering this machine when a light bulb lit up in my head, and I took the trouble to measure the corridor and access to the Utility Room - problem. It would fit where we intended, but we could not *actually* get it to where it was intended. Shades of my wonderful office work top.

Back to the drawing board, and various people said they had a twin-tub machine designed for caravans. Much searching on t'interweb and we found just the thing - a twin tub, 240V but only 130W consumption, and most importantly it was light weight and small enough to be manoeuvred into position without demolishing the internal walls in Hekla. So that is what we have, an olde stylee twin tub machine which does the job. Not as convenient as an automatic, but we could get by, and the bedding and towels we could manage at launderettes when we were close to them.

Anyway, back to the (then) present, and our 2 day mooring was a productive one. We had picked up a pallet at some stage on our journey and it was of such a design that is sat firmly on Hekla's curved roof, so rather than break it up for kindling we earmarked it as somewhere to store wood on the roof. We had also fished out of the cut a long 6 inch by half inch plank, and I set to with my (t)rusty saw and hammer and nails and built box sides for our pallet. We were starting to take on the regulation patina of itinerant live-aboard boaters with a variety of 'stuff' on the roof, whereby the snobby shiny boaters can readily identify people of 'our sort' and snub their noses at us and generally act all superior. (or should that be superfluous?) Anyway, we definitely felt like we were 'going bosky' and fitting in like the natives.

Our 2 days done we got itchy tiller fingers again and set off once more, landing up at Stone - The self-styled Canal Town - home to Terry Darlington of Narrow Dog fame, and also the oldest narrowboat hire company in the country. My log entry for that day was simply "We like Stone." It is a compact and pretty town and really embraces the canal as it passes through. A single old fashioned high street - and like many small towns, having a good range of Charity Shops for us to browse, as well as a Morrisons supermarket where we could stock up on alcohol and other supplies.

[36] - Gulper Pump - another quirk of life on a narrowboat. Sink drains are generally not a problem because the sink is above the waterline and a normal domestic style drain works fine. The Shower, on the other hand, obviously the shower tray in on the floor. The floor is some 18 inches below the waterline. You cannot simply fit a plug hole and drain it outside. Bailing it out would be a bit of a pain in the bum, frankly, so most narrowboats with a shower have these quaintly named Gulper pumps, so called because of the noise they make. Because the water from a shower is not a huge volume a normal pump would probably burn out sucking air through it, so these devilishly clever devises pulse and the noise they make is just like a gulping sound - actually I think they sound more like Gollum from the hobbit, - gollum……gollum……gollum…….gollum - but I suppose the marketing droids would not think a Gollum Pump would have that same snappy ring to it.

A Bit Of a Diversion

Leaving Stone the next day we laboured our way up the many locks out of the town under dull grey and chilly skies and wound our way through Stoke on Trent, having passed the Wedgewood factory on the Southern outskirts. Stoke is OK, I suppose, but on a dull cold April day it came across as a bit, erm, rough at the edges? I don't want to upset any locals (what *do* residents of Stoke call themselves?) but in sharp contrast to Stone just to the South, Stoke is a bit post-industrial in places. There are interesting spots to explore, like Trentham Gardens, for example, and some fascinating industrial archaeology to see along the way, but it left us feeling a little but underwhelmed, and we did *not* fancy stopping overnight there.

However that is just what we ended up doing. When we arrived at Etruria we decided that we could not resist a little detour up the Caldon Canal - raved over by many as a beautiful canal to visit - all be it a dead-end and having to retrace your steps.

So after Etruria lock, the last lock rising from Stoke, we made the awkward right turn - it is about 120 degrees - into Etruria Basin, and as it was getting a bit late and there were several locks to negotiate, including a double staircase lock immediately out of the basin, we moored up for the night outside the Etruria Industrial Museum - which was, and stayed, resolutely closed. Apparently it only opens on special occasions and the odd weekend, because it is run by local volunteers.

Despite being in 'The Bad Lands' as we had dire warnings from other boaters, we spent a peaceful night there, and the dogs had plenty of space to run riot in and burn off some of their energies.

Next morning, bright sunshine, and we set off up the staircase lock and wound our way through The Potteries, past the ubiquitous bottle shaped kilns - mostly restored as display pieces, some integrated into new architecture, or some simply crumbling though neglect. The canal wound a tortuous and shallow route - on one occasion we met another boat coming towards us, we moved to the left and promptly ran aground. One bridge in particular was so low we didn't think we would make it under it without scraping the paint off the roof.

Then we spotted the Bridgewater Pottery - Lesley had heard of Emma Bridgewater's work though university, so we had to tied up and go and explore. We had a wander through the factory shop, mostly exclaiming "How Much?" at the prices on some (most) of the pieces. We would need a 2nd mortgage if we wanted to replace all Hekla's crockery there.   Back on the boat we were treated to the spectacle of a skip wheeled out of the factory and a bloke methodically throwing tea pots as hard as he could into another larger skip making sure each one was smashed beyond recognition - Extreme Quality Control or what? No such thing as 'seconds' from the Bridgewater factory.

We were definitely in The Bad Lands of Hanley here though - a high brick wall to one side with lots of graffiti and empty beer cans on the towpath, so we pressed on through the very industrial and suburban scenery, under a few lift bridges and up the lone Engine lock and the four locks at Stockton Brook, the rare sight of a traffic island in the middle of the cut with a Keep Left road sign on it at Stanley Moss, finally calling it a day above the Hazelhurst locks at the junction where the Caldon bifurcates (ooh. That sounds painful.) into the Froghall and Leek arms.

Looking on a map Leek is to the right and Froghall to the left, but oddly the Leek arm branches to the right while the Froghall line carries straight on down a flight of locks, then passes *under* the Leek arm which turns vaguely North East while the Froghall arm meanders vaguely South East.

The next day we meandered our way to the end - ish. The canal terminates at present in Froghall Basin, which is at the other end of a short very low tunnel. We could have cleared everything off Hekla's roof and made it, but we walked to the end instead, it's very nice in parts, once you get over the site of a large demolished works right by the canal, but the effort to sail Hekla those last couple of hundred yards was not really worth it.

If Froghall Basin is a bit on the underwhelming side, the route to get there could hardly be any more different. After Cheddleton the canal is accompanied by the Churnet Valley railway, and there can be nothing more satisfying than cruising along though deep wooded valleys with steam trains puffing by on the tracks paralleling the canal. At Oakmeadowford lock (try saying that after a pint or three.) the canal joins the River Churnet for a mile or so until Consal Forge, where it departs once more over a weir and the canal turns left under another *very* low bridge and the railway station platform on the down line (or is it the up line - I get confused) is actually built out over the canal on wooden struts.

This whole area is picture postcard country. If you have a narrowboat you should seriously brave the Bad Lands in Stoke and explore it. If you don't have a narrowboat you should make the effort to visit the Churnet Valley railway and explore it by steam train. Perhaps calling at the delightful canal side pub the Holly Bush at Denford just after the Leek arm junction and in the shadow of the aqueduct carrying the Leek arm over the Froghall arm.

The only downside (if you can call it such) is that the canal is deep down in the twisting wooded valley carved by the Churnet, and there is no TV, Mobile phone or broadband connection to be had anywhere along the upper reaches. (Stop Press - a return visit 2 years later and we had a full broadband signal on our 3 MiFi unit - but still no TV signal, and, oddly no phone signal either!)

On the return trip we moored at Cheddleton and our friend and mentor Tony Haynes came to meet us and see Hekla for the first time. Tony had sold Dreamcatcher a few years earlier and with the proceeds he had bought himself a Hymer mobile home and continues to explore the inland waterways system in it. He brought his latest Mrs Drifter with him, and we met at the Red Lion pub just by the canal. It was a Sunday and the plan was to have a meal in the pub that evening - however the pub had other ideas and after their Sunday Lunch session they did not do food on Sunday evenings.

So we had beers and went back to Hekla, where Lesley did a wonderful five loaves and seven fishes act with the tiny beef joint we had bought for our Sunday meal before Tony announced he was coming. Somehow she managed to stretch it out between four of us and we had a most pleasant meal in the candle lit cosy cabin of Hekla.

Tony had sweet talked the landlord of the Red Lion and they stayed the night in the Hymer in the pub car park, and the next day we all explored the fine restored Cheddleton Flint Mill. Another must see if/when you visit the area. The mill is actually working on the open days and the waterwheel powers the machinery with the local volunteers demonstrating things and giving an insight into the workings in its heyday.

Tony & Di took their leave and we decided to stay over for another day of rest. There are a couple of shops in the local village - and as per the usual rule of shops and canals, they are about ½ mile up a steep hill.

After our day off we continued our Westward course and stopped for the night near Stockton Brook so that we could make the trip through the Bad Land in one go the next day. We were on the edge of the Six Towns conurbation, bordering onto the Staffordshire hills, It had been dull grey and raining when we set off that morning, but by the time we moored for the night the sun had come out and all was bright and cheerful with the world once more.

It was at that night mooring that I came over all poetic at the scene from my smoking room.

"Tonight's smoking room view.
No camera can do justice to this.
I stand at the back of Hekla; it is like living on the surface of a mirror.
The trees reflected in the glass-smooth surface of the still waters.
In the near distance a ridge, festooned with a garland of orange and white lights.
Sometimes a cruise is like a grand tour of England's back gardens, the scruffy, the ordinary, and the fabulous.
But I would not exchange our ever changing view of their back gardens with their static view of our canal.

116

We really are living the dream, and I sometimes pity those who can not share in our un-reality."

Next day we continued back to the end of the Caldon at Etruria and back on to the Trent and Mersey main line. Ahead of us was the dreaded Harecastle Tunnel, but we could not make it to the entrance in time for the last passage through that day, so we moored up by Westport Lake in Stoke for the night and set off for the tunnel the next morning.

The Harecastle Tunnel is another canal icon. At nearly 2 miles long it was an engineering marvel at the time it was first constructed by James Brindley in 1777, but as the canals got busier it became a bottleneck and Thomas Telford was engaged to build another tunnel alongside the Brindley tunnel which was opened in 1827 - taking 'only' 3 years to construct, and the two tunnels operated as a two-lane system. Over the years mining subsidence has sunk the original Brindley tunnel so much that is was abandoned, but you can still see the opening to it by the side of the Telford tunnel.

You arrive at the Southern portal of the tunnel to find an imposing structure at the entrance, and a CaRT attendant who gives you a short lecture and an information sheet for your trip through. The tunnel is only wide enough for one boat, so there are attendants at either end and boats are sent though in convoys - each boat separated from the next by a 10 minute gap so that you are not choking to death on the exhaust fumes of the boat in front.

On this particular day we had a long wait before we could go through. Not because there was a convoy of boats heading South, but, this being The Bad Lands after all, someone had driven a car into the canal at the Northern portal. We later learned that is was a nearly new Ford Ranger truck stolen during the night from a nearby farm and the wags who done the deed thought it was a jolly wheeze to dump it in the canal. We had to wait while it was recovered, so we sat and drank tea and chatted to the CaRT attendant and the other boaters for a couple of hours - thankfully in relatively warm spring sunshine.

The huge imposing structure at the tunnel portal is actually housing a huge set of extractor fans. Once we are given the all clear from the Northern end the gates are swung open and we were first in the queue of 3 boats to enter the dark and mysterious underworld. Once the last boat is through the gates are closed behind us shutting off the dwindling circle of daylight astern and the fans start up. The sound is very loud and disconcerting - a pair of huge turbines sucking air through the tunnel, you can feel the breeze immediately.

Ahead we can see a teeny tiny white dot - the Northern portal. Hekla's twin headlights illuminate the tunnel sides and roof, and we each carry torches to help and to look at the walls and roof as we pass. At some point you need to keep a look out for The Boggart which haunts the tunnel. However mostly you need to keep a lookout for bloody ice cold water pouring out of the roof. It takes around 30 to 40 minutes to travel the length, and it is a test of concentration for the person at the tiller to avoid zigzagging along banging from one side to the other.

Of course I managed a perfect passage straight as an arrow from one end to the other <cough cough>

Emerging at last from the stygian gloom into the sunshine we resume our discussion about our route across the top of England. We had a choice of 3 - the Leeds-Liverpool, the Rochdale, or the Huddersfield Narrow canal - including yet another iconic canal landmark, the Standedge Tunnel.

The Huddersfield route was definitely the shorter of the three, and towpath wisdom has it that it should be tackled sooner rather than later, because with the transfer of the waterways from British Waterways to the Canal and River Trust as a charity, if funds get tight the Huddersfield route may be one of the early casualties due to reducing maintenance.

And so as we climbed out of the Potteries we turned left onto the Macclesfield canal before Bulls Bridge - another quirky canal junction whereby the canal turns left, the main line drops through the first of the Heartbreak hill locks, and the Macclesfield canal swings East crossing over the Trent & Mersey canal via an aqueduct, followed shortly by another ubiquitous Stop Lock at Hall Green where 2 canal companies preserved 'their' water with a lock which usually has a fall of a couple of inches.

We filled up with fuel at Heritage Narrowboats and continued on our way along what was a very pretty and rural canal - a welcome change after The Bad Lands, and found ourselves at Congleton - well just past it - on an embankment with fine views to both sides - to our left (towpath side) was a steep valley with a stream running through under an impressive high arched railway viaduct, while to the offside we had views across the Cheshire countryside. It is at times like this when you really appreciate boating, with such scenery outside your every window, what is not to like?

We took the dogs down into the valley for exercise and to explore. Max had been kept inside when we cruised after the dramatic episode on the Shroppie on our first cruise, so we let him loose in the stream and he had a whale of a time splashing about, finding deep pools to swim in, and generally being, well, just our own happy Maxwell puppy dog. (At 14 years old he could still act the puppy, and we still thought of him as a puppy)

It was a fine spring day and we climbed the far side of the valley and came out onto a track on a disused railway line which took us back to the canal at the far end of the embankment. There was a small wharf on the off side from us and a couple of itinerant live aboard boats were moored there, one of them by the name of King Coal. The crews were typical old-hippy or old rocker types and it looked like a very cosy little set up they had in their private offside mooring spot. The next morning they set off and passed us with the bloke sat on the cabin side cheerfully singing in a loud lustful voice "Old King Cole Was A Merry Old Soul........."

We set off ourselves shortly after, and again the day was bright and sunny. Then we got to our first real locks on the Macclesfield (I don't really count the stop lock as a proper lock) and I got off to set the first lock of the Bosley flight of 11 locks - and the skies clouded over, and the rain began - proper North West rain it was, the kind that gets you wet. By the time Hekla was raising in the lock I was completely soaked to the skin, and we were committed to the whole Bosley flight. It was not cold, and it was not worth getting inside to dry off and change into dry clothing nor was it worth putting a waterproof coat on - as I was already soaking, so I plodded up the locks, gradually feeling more and more miserable and sorry for myself.

We finally reached the top lock, and the only moorings other than the lock landing were "Permit Holders Only" - but the first one was empty, so we said "Sod It" and tied ourselves up there - we had the odd dirty look from a bloke on one of the other Permit Holder boats, but nothing was said. There is a good CaRT service facility there, with toilets, shower and Elsan point and there was even a washing machine - but they needed a CaRT card to operate - pity, I could have done with a nice long hot shower at that point. It was only later that we discovered that the showers at **all** the CaRT facilities are free - and had been for some time. It was just that they had not got around to removing the card machine and there was no sign to say it was not needed. Oh well. One day I promise myself we are going to go back there and have a bloody free hot shower.

The next day we set off once more and got to Bollington, where I had arranged for our daughter Vicky to come over and meet us as I had to go to see a customer over in Lincoln. It turned out to be a day for bumping into people.

Bimbling along the cut we passed Here Be Dragons and Kitt, a Facebook friend of Lesley's shouted out. We pulled in to the side and they did and Lesley jumped off and had a long towpath talk with Kitt, who she had never met in Real Life before and they got on like a house on fire. Then we moored up on the embankment at Bollington and who should we meet but Stella and Chris, another pair of facebook friends on their boat Grace.

They had broken down. RCR had come out and replaced their starter motor, which promptly burst into flames. So they were stuck at Bollington for a week waiting for a replacement starter motor - hence they had no means of generating electricity so were using torches and candles, and no way to get the water out of the boat water tank. They had a couple of large plastic containers they trundled over the bridge to the tap to fill up. We had a small generator and we offered to loan it to them to at lease charge their batteries up enough for the water pump to work, but they declined our offer, saying they were fine 'roughing it'.

They had only bought and moved onto their boat the previous August and had no end of mechanical issues with Grace - all more or less sorted by now, thankfully, but it was a baptism of fire for them as they were completely new to boating and had taken the plunge to move aboard Grace and were basically picking it up as they went along.

Vicky arrived later that day and we drove back to her house in Bardney where I slept in our caravan in their garden. We had a successful meeting with a new prospective customer the next day and won a decent order for a new system, then we drove back to Hekla at Bollington and Vicky stayed with us until Friday.

We arrived at Marple Junction and took the left turn down the locks into Dukinfied and the junction with the Ashton and Huddersfield Narrow canal - only we didn't *quite* do this.

As we made the tight turn to the first lock there was an almighty banging and clattering below my feet and we lost power. Opening the rear deck hatch revealed that the bolts connecting the drive coupling to the gearbox - the ones that disappeared back in Atherstone, had gone walkabout again.

Obviously the 2nd hand bolts I had got from the garage at Atherstone were not up to the job. This time I fished them out of the bilge with my trusty magnet onna stick and re-tightened them, but a more permanent solution was definitely on the cards. There is a boatyard at Dukinfield, so perhaps they have something there?

We finally descended the locks and Vicky took her leave and got a bus back to the car at Bollington and went home, leaving us to our own devices.

This entire section of the Macclesfield and Peak Forest canals is very pleasant indeed, and surprisingly so entering Manchester through leafy cuttings you are hardly aware that you are in the Greater Manchester Conurbation, passing through Romiley and

Hyde, under the M67 motorway and a pleasant spot just before the junction with a country park by the canal.

In the morning I walked around to the boatyard to see if they had suitable bolts to replace the ones on the prop coupling - no they didn't. However. They said I could get them from Frances Kirk in Denton. Wow. A blast from the past or what? Back in the 1970's I worked for an engineering suppliers and Kirks were one of our competitors. This whole scene was like Déjà Vu. Passing factories, and this sites of ex factories that were customers back when Manchester had a thriving engineering and manufacturing sector. To be honest I was surprised Frances Kirk still existed. But they did, and the bloke from the boatyard said he lived near there, and would drive me over - I could get the bus back.

And so we drove into deepest darkest South Manchester - Frances Kirk was a revelation. Swanky new building in an industrial estate, not only did they provide me with half a dozen 10x30mm high tensile stainless steel bolts, but also a bottle of the correct Loctite product to make sure they did not go a wandering again. And all for a whopping 5 quid.

My driver hung around while I did the deal, and dropped me off near Sainsburys supermarket where he said I could easily get a bus back to Portland Basin where Lesley, the dogs and Hekla were waiting for me. However - a teensy bit of a problem. I generally have a very good sense of direction - except in Manchester.

The place seems to me to be just a chaotic jumble of places and roads, none of which are notable with the exception of the motorways. Even the A6 arrives at Stockport then mysteriously reappears North of Manchester and where it goes in between is a complete mystery. The A57 I know, because it is a major route sort-of from my home town of St Helens and Lincoln, passing within a hole in a bug's nadger of Tuxford where we had lived for 20-odd years.

The rest is a vague mess in my brain-compass. So I had a bit of a wander, found a bus stop, had no idea where on earth I was supposed to be going to, so I wandered back to Sainsburys and found a taxi-phone by the exit and called for a cab. It took some explaining to the taxi driver as to where, exactly, I need to go, and I suspect his brain-compass was as confused as mine when it comes to Manchester, because we ended up at a dead end road in a grotty industrial estate vaguely in the same vicinity of where I had left Hekla moored up. As it happens I did spot a bridge over the canal - with bollards to stop cars going over it, and said "this will do." and handed over a fiver for the fare and finally got back to Hekla clutching my shiny High Tensile Stainless Steel prizes.

Journey to the Centre of the Earth

Bolts duly bolted and loctited into place we are ready to climb up the Pennines on the Huddersfield Narrow Canal - henceforth to be called the Uddersfield Shallow Canal.

At they summit is the dread Standedge Tunnel. And you can not just rack up one day and go through it, you have to book a passage in advance via CaRT. At over 3 miles long it can take 2 hours or so to get through, and it is one way, so passage is restricted to 3 (or in our case 4) boats per day in alternate directions on alternate days. So we were booked in for our passage on the 5th May at 11:00 a.m. We had 2 days to cover 10 miles and 31 locks.

The start of the canal is a tad underwhelming - urban decay and pollution at its worst. The canal winds its was through the more depressed areas of Ashton-Under-Lyne, at one point we passed an entire area of streets demolished and cleared, and it was eerie to see the cobbled streets in a grid, pavements in place, but just flat compacted rubble where the houses used to be. Lots of detritus floating in the canal and accumulating by the locks - not the prettiest of places until the canal finally rises and becomes the focal point and a part of the High Street in Stalybridge.

From here the canal resumes its leafy seclusion as it relentlessly climbs up the Western flanks of the Pennines, and of course Manchester lived up to its nickname The Rainy City and we were soaking and chilled by the time we called it a day at Roaches Lock. We should really have persevered and made it to Uppermill/Saddleworth which is a nice spot with varied pubs, café's and shops, but the light was fading and we were just too exhausted and a little depressed by the day to continue any further.

The next day was another dull and grey morning, though thankfully not raining - yet. and we untied and continued on up the hills, under the imposing Saddleworth Viaduct as the TransPennine railway crosses high above, we paused at Uppermill for a brief explore and supplies before pressing on -

we had to be at the summit at Diggle by the next morning, and we still had 12 locks to work over the next mile to the summit.

Here is where the canal really earns its alter-ego title of the Huddersfield Shallow - Hekla was dragging her bottom across every pound, and I had to keep letting more water down to avoid grounding - which obviously makes the next pound even worse. The locks are close together, so I was walking up the Pennines and bench-pressing somewhere in the region of 90 Tons of lock gates at the same time - and the rain came back with a vengeance, and the wind, and the temperature took a dive. Every pound was a struggle, and every lock was a chore, as we finally reached the last lock - appropriately named Summit Lock - and tied up for the night. I more or less staggered into the warmth of Hekla's cabin.

I *really* needed that stiff whisky.

And yet perversely we enjoyed it! The weather, the grind across shallow pounds, the sometimes horizontal rain - but we were dressed suitably and did not get soaked through, and the vistas across the valleys and the moors were ample compensation for the struggle - so don't be put off tackling this canal! It **is** hard work, sure, and in bad weather it is even harder, but the rewards are worth the effort - and it does not *always* rain on the western flanks of the Pennines. Mostly, true, but it isn't a universal rule, so you may be lucky. Anyway, we survived to tell the tale and reached our destination in time for our underground adventure the next day.

Normally we believe that only 3 boats per day are in the trip through the tunnel, but there were already 3 boats moored up when we arrived, so we were a little bit perturbed, given past experience of other people's organisation skills having problems sorting out a piss up in a brewery, but the next day we will see - for tonight food and plenty of wine and whisky to recover from the long cold wet uphill slog of the previous 2 days.

After the cold, wind and rain so far, dawn the next morning brought clear blue skies and sunshine. And we were scheduled to spend a large chunk of it underground.

Our 2 sons Ross & Mike and our daughter Vicky all said they wanted to come through the tunnel with us, so they drove over in 2 cars, parking one at the Yorkshire end at Marsden and ferrying over to the Lancashire side at Diggle.

We wandered down to the tunnel portal and chatted to the other boaters waiting for their passage. Of the three 2 of them were fine, open, friendly, as is usual on the cut - especially outside the main 'season' - the exception being the first boat by the tunnel portal. It was *Shiny*. It looked like it had just come out of the builders, absolutely pristine paintwork, gleaming brass work and all ropes neatly coiled 'just so' It was crewed by a pair of middle-aged couples all four with matching blues sweatshirts with 'Thrupp Cruising Club' emblazoned on them. They were just a bit uncommunicative, and to my cheery smile and Good Morning I received a mechanical *click* smile *click* off response. Oh well, you encounter all sorts on the canals.

Our CaRT chaperones turned up - three of them. Like I said, we were a bit worried at there being 3 boats here already. - but they assured me it was not a problem, we were booked in OK, and the chaperone on the first boat through would be driving back over the top to take us through - Phew. The next hurdle is being measured up for fit. The have a special device - well a pole with a cross bar on it - to check that the overall height of the boat and assorted roof detritus will fit though the lowest point in the tunnel - we were fine *except* for the fire wood on the roof, and one particularly hefty log had to be lifted down and put in the bows - more on that bit of wood later.

As it turned out it was a bit fortunate that we were 4th in the queue as Mike and Ross were late. Mike uses satnav, and *always* has a problem coming over to see us, either going for a grand circular tour of Stockport if he comes over the Pennines or ending up on the M6 toll if he comes across the middle route. This time they had a scenic tour of the sights of Stockport - passing some landmarks several times before finding their way. Those of you with more than a sketchy grasp of geography will have noted that Stockport is not, in fact, on the route from Nottinghamshire to Diggle on the Pennines - no mater, Mike can get lost on his way upstairs to his bedroom.

All's well that ends well and they finally turned up with ½ hour to spare.

Our chaperone gave us a brief, erm, briefing about the procedure in the tunnel. Only the steerer would be allowed on the stern with the chaperone, everyone else must be in the boat - we took this to mean it was OK to stand in the bows, because Lesley and our 3 offspring did not really fancy sitting in the cabin with the light on for the duration of the trip. There are, in actually fact, 4 tunnels through the hill, 3 railway tunnels as well as the canal tunnel. One of the railway tunnels is disused and acts as a maintenance tunnel. In the early days a BW employee would shadow the boats along the service tunnel in a land rover. At three points on the journey there are 'Addits' - access tunnels across the 4 bores for maintenance and emergencies.

When the tunnel was re-opened on 2001 most of the trains were diesel and ventilation was an issue, so boats were not allowed through under their own power, and were towed through in a chain by and electric tug. The boats were covered in rubber sheeting to protect them and all crews sat in the tug boat.

Today the lines are electric, so the issue with boat diesels adding to the general fug from the train diesels is vastly reduced, even so the chaperone has a gas detector and alarm with him and we were issued with hard hats in a rather fetching shade of yellow to keep things tickety-boo with the Elfin Safe Tea bods.

Mark - for that was our CaRT chaperone's name (well it wasn't but its shorter to type Mark than 'our chaperone') - said that we would be stopping off at each of the addits so that he could phone home to reassure the other end that we hadn't broken down, been buried in a roof collapse, or succumbed to noxious vapours. I was steering, but Ross wanted a go as well, so we agreed that Ross could take over at the third addit - Mark said it was an easier stretch from there to the end, and the first and middle bits were a bit, erm, challenging, so required someone with the most experience at the helm. Especially for the S bends…………. - *The What*?

At last Mark's phone rang and he was given the OK to set off - and into the depths of The Mines of Moria we plunged.

At first it is all a bit mundane, just the usual brick lined arched tunnel - then it opens out and it is like one of those river rides or ghost trains you used to get at funfairs, with the roof and walls all spray lined with concrete and you feel you are travelling through the burrow of some giant worm. Mark explained that when they restored the tunnel this section was all gritstone and crumbling so it was lined with steel mesh and spray concrete. At other places the tunnel opens our to bare rock, sometimes the sides are so close there are inches to spare, at others it opens out and you are in a large cavern.

Mark explained that when they first cut the tunnel over 200 years ago all they had was blasting powder and pick and shovel, so when they set a charge it would either go **BANG** - or just *phutt* so trying to keep a straight course with rudimentary tools materials and equipment - its amazing they even managed at all.   Travelling West to East you only get to see the visitor centre once you have done it - and there is a schematic showing the *intended* route - a red arrow-straight line - and the *actual* route - straight as a dogs back leg.

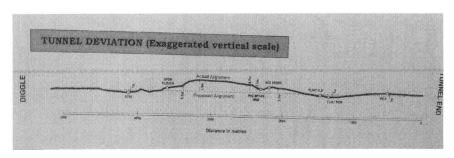

In the bows Lesley was filming it on her smartphone - but was getting annoyed when one or other of them frequently exclaimed "Oh for Fuck Sake" as Hekla barely cleared the jagged boulders either side. Then we came to the S bend - bloody hair raising when your headlights are illuminating a solid rock wall dead ahead as the water jinks to the right then to the left.

At the first addit Mark jumped off - I said "Its a shame there is no smoking - I could *really* do with a ciggie right now" - No

128

Problem says he. I'm having one. And he lit up a cig standing in the addit by the side of the boat.

At the third addit I swapped places with Ross - he put on my hard hat and life jacket and I retreated to the bows - and was a passenger for the last third of the journey. Ross took over and was mortified when at yet another tight pinch point with jaggedy sticky out rocky bits he managed to scrape the front starboard side navigation light off. (He still hasn't bought us the promised replacement to this day. <hint hint>)

For an insight into the experience there as some good photographs on the excellent Pennine Waterways web site at: http://www.penninewaterways.co.uk/huddersfield/standedge6.htm

As we were last through of four boats and mooring is limited at the Marsden end we were told we could moor up outside the trip-boat base & café right by the tunnel portal - with the proviso that we would have to move before 10:00 a.m. as the trip boats would then need the space for the landing stage.

Before the kids drove home we all wandered down the towpath to Marsden to The Railway pub right by the canal and the first lock on the Yorkshire side descent. <Techy aside> All the locks on the West side are numbered in ascending order with a W suffix, those on the East side are numbered in descending order, rather imaginatively with an E suffix. Our last lock in Lancashire was 32W, the first lock in Yorkshire was 42E. Anyway, putting the aside behind us we had a meal with Ross, Mike and Vicky, - and a bonus, they even let us bring the dogs in with us. After the meal and a couple of drinks (non-alcoholic for Mike and Vicky as designated drivers) we ambled back to Hekla.

Remember the shiny boat at back at the entrance to the tunnel that morning? Well we shouldn't really laugh - well, OK, we might have smirked a bit - it was moored outside the pub, and it had a *lot* of scratches and scrapes along its pristine paintwork. The two blokes were sat at the back looking thoroughly pissed off, and the two women were sat at the front having a right old rant about their husbands for scratching their shiny paintwork.

Back at the Hekla we said our goodbyes to the kids as they set off for home. This is where that log of wood that we had to lift off the roof back at Diggle comes back into the tale, as Lesley stepped onto the boat she put her foot on it and it slid away and Lesley came crashing down landing awkwardly on the bow locker across her back. So I had a semi-crippled wife to care for over the next week or so.

I got chatting to Mike, the bloke on the boat just before us going through that morning. He was single handed, so the locks up and down the Pennines must have been a lot worse for him than for me. He told us he was heading for his new mooring at Shireoaks on the Chesterfied canal. He lived on his boat and had been cruising on the Macclesfield canal, he had 2 sons and was separated from his wife, so he had custody one week in two and they went to school in Sheffield, so he had taken the mooring at Shireoaks as being easier to drive them to school each morning when he had them. We told him that we were going to get a mooring at Shireoaks but it fell through, but we were heading for the Chesterfield ourselves and would look him up when we got there. (You will have to watch out for the sequel to find the results of *that* particular plan though.)

Next morning we were rudely disturbed by the trip boat crew demanding we move at the unreasonable hour of 9:00 a.m.. barely time for my 2nd cup of tea. So we fired up and moved down to the now vacant mooring by the pub while Lesley was recovering from her fall, and I walked down the hill into Marsden for supplies - and what a pleasant little town it is. Lesley was a bit put out that she was missing it so we stayed over another night and the next morning Lesley hobbled down with me to explore some more, and browse the very bohemian food shop on the high street.

The walk was helping with her back - keeping moving in these situations is often the best medicine, although she was flagging a bit by the time we got back up the steep hill to the boat, but we had bought some Voltarol from the chemists and that was also helping to ease the pain. Giving her a piggy-back up the hill did my own back no good at all, mind.

It's all down hill from here.

Eventually Lesley had recovered enough for us to set off once more, this time I would be walking *down* the Pennines but still bench-pressing around 160 tons of lock gates - and, as it happened, wading a lot. (I know it is about 160 tons because the locks are helpfully numbered in descending order from lock 41e at Marsden so 41 locks to go, each having a top gate weighing around 2 tons, and 2 bottom gates weighing about a ton each.)

Our chaperone though the tunnel had given us a sage bit of advice:
"If you can see the next lock, walk to it, empty it and open the top paddles before you empty your own lock. Otherwise you will flood the towpath."

So we did - and did it make any difference? Not one jot. Every short pound between the locks required me to wade through a flood of Biblical Proportions to get to the next lock. OK for me because I swapped my boots for wellies, but the gongoozlers on the towpath were doing a Queen Victoria. (oh all right! "We are *Not* Amused!")

Never mind. Only 11 of them to get through before we could look for somewhere to tie up away from the accusing glare of the wet-footed gongoozlers. And so below the delightfully named Pig Tail lock we pulled over to the side, ground up the silt, reversed a bit and tried again, until we could get to the side-ish, whereupon I promptly slipped and fell in.

Once you have all *quite* finished laughing at me, let me disillusion you on one score. This was not like my falling in at Nottingham on the river Trent (details of which you will have to sit on your hands and wait for the next book) rather the Huddersfield Narrow Canal was living up to its alter-ego of the Huddersfield Shallow Canal and I was stood up to my knees in the cut - my kneeses being less than 2'3" above my footses, accounts for the reason we could not get Hekla's 2'3" draught to the side properly.

So after a quiet night we set off at the crack of mid-morning to continue our down hill progress looking forward to the delights of Slaithwaite. (Pronounced, apparently, Slowit - at least the locals do, but as a friend of mine discovered when he was trying to be clever and asked for a train ticker to Slowit, he was met with total blank incomprehension until he repeated his request for a ticket to Slay-thwait)

Only we didn't quite get there, as the novel guillotine lock 24e (where the gate is a steel barrier that rises vertically like a, well, like a guillotine, really) was semi-broken and padlocked to prevent us mere boaters from operating it, and a notice informing us that we had to phone the CaRT office to arrange for someone to come and un-padlock it and operate it for us. (Presumably so that if it broke while we were passing under the guillotine bit and it guillotined us we (or our next of kin) would have someone to take to court.)

However this was Sunday. CaRT offices only open weekdays - and Monday was a bank holiday as well. So we had to moor up above the lock and wait a full day until the men in blue t-shirts and lifejackets could come and job the job to get us through the lock on Tuesday. Fortunately our New Best Friend Mike, who you may remember we met at Standedge, was also stuck there as well.

Just to add to the idyllic scene we discovered that the semi-broken lock 24e was also leaking badly. A fact brought home to us I couple of hours after we had moored up when we noticed things kept rolling to one side, and we were running aground and listing heavily to port. The only answer was to walk back to the next lock above - Shaker Wood lock 25e and *just* crack open a top and bottom paddle to let enough water down to compensate for the leak in the guillotine lock. Not something that is strictly advisable, but one handy trait of the intrepid narrowboater is to learn to cope with the unexpected and to improvise as you go. It was either that or watch as Hekla and Mike's boat gradually settled lower and lower and at an increasingly alarming angle onto the canal bed.

Fortunately it was less than half a mile walk into Slaithwaite/Slowit so we went for an explore. We had been before but only on a flying visit, detouring from the main

Huddersfield road above one day simply out of curiosity, but at canal life pace it is a wonderful little gem of a typical Northern small town (well, more like a big village really) with lots of independent shops and a butchers selling yet another "Best Pork Pies In The World" - when any fule knoze the Best Pork Pies In The World are to be had on a Saturday Morning from Birchalls Butchers in St Helens (where me Mam used to work) It has to be a Saturday as the pies are even more unctuous and flavoursome because they keep all the scraps from the bacon slicer tray during the week and add them to the filling mix - there are queueueues outside the door on any Saturday.

But I am getting ahead of myself here. The more astute reader may recall we arrived at the 'closed until Tuesday' lock on a Sunday - and in fact most of the shops were closed, so we only did the window-shopping bit until CaRT came and released us on Tuesday and we moored up in the town for the night to explore in more detail.

More detail included the absolutely delightful Slaithwaite/Slowit Emporium - a veritable Aladdin's cave of curiosities, brick-a-brac, Auntie Queues and Vintage clothing. Lesley bought a nice silk Chinese print jacket, but my absolute delight could not be hidden when I found a Parka.

As a youth I had a scooter - a proper one, a Lambretta GP150 (bored out to 175cc) with crash bars, mirrors, spotlights, front & rear chrome racks, *two* backrests - with those old fashioned car headrests you used to get that slipped over car seat backs, but attached to the back rests with 18" chrome mirror stalks and jubly clips. I never owned a Parka though - being a pull-the-door-marked-push kind of person even then, I was into Rock music rather than the usual Tamla Motown stuff, and I wore purple jeans, tie dyed T shirts and a **huge** RAF great coat as my preferred biking Haute Couture.

So chuffed was I that when I tried it on I kept it on as we continued to browse, and the jolly lady proprietor remarked rather loudly to me "Excuse me. But we are *trying* to attract a refined clientele in this establishment." - as she struggled to conceal the big grin across here face.

The Bonus was that my prized Parka only cost me a Tenner. Bargain. I also scored a nice pair of large round John Lennon style sunglasses - perfect for our developing Steam Punk personas.

What's that? The Pies? Oh yes, we did sample them, and yes, they were delicious - not as good as a Saturday Special Birchalls pork pie, but passable for a Yorkshire palate I suppose.

After a quiet night we set off once more down the hills. The countryside around the canal which had been pretty along the steep sided valley slowly started to become more and more urban as the ribbon of relatively flat land was exploited to build houses factories and warehouses. Still pleasant enough, mind, and we had a nature interlude at one lock 4e when Lesley spotted a water vole desperately trying to climb the foot or so of vertical lock wall to get out - I risked life and limb and put my hand under this vicious wild animal and gently gave it a pog up the wall, where I swear it paused and turned, looked at me with an unspoken 'thanks' and scampered off into the deep grass.

As previously mentioned, the locks and bridges are all numbered in descending order with an e suffix for East, which meant that the next lock being 22e we knew we had 22 locks to go through before the Huddersfield Narrow transformed as if by magic into the Huddersfield Broad canal at … yes, Huddersfield. Which we could not actually get to, on account of when we got to Milnsbridge someone had managed to completely drain the pound below lock 7e by opening the paddles on lock 6e during the night.

There was a boat already moored at the lock, and they told us that they had informed CaRT and someone was on their way. A pair of Men In Blue duly arrived and after much sucking of teeth told us they would be letting water down from the locks above, but it would be the next morning before there would be enough water down for us to *just* get through the pound to the offending lock. So we settled in for the night - to be joined by another 2 boats before dark, so 4 of us waiting for the morning - which arrived cool and damp, and, as we discovered when we strolled down the towpath, a still empty pound. Whoever had done the deed had obviously returned in the night and done the deed again as an encore.

We checked the paddles on lock 6e and they had been opened just enough to let the water out slowly - obviously done by hand without a windlass, but just enough to do the damage, so we closed them up and waited. The Men In Blue turned up around 07:30 and after yet more sucking of teeth and muttering, said they would let more water down and keep an eye on the level and would let us through as soon as there was enough water in the centre channel to keep us afloat.

I don't know if you have ever seen a canal drained of most of its water, but it can be an interesting sight as the detritus thrown in by uncaring locals gets exposed. There are the ubiquitous empty beer bottles and cans, perhaps a couple of shopping trolleys, the odd rusting bicycle, maybe even a motorbike, occasionally whole cars. But how on Ged's earth had a large and *very* heavy cube of crushed car got where it was, half way between 2 locks with no vehicular access for a hundred yards or more. I mean one of those cubes you get when those giant crushing machines swallow a car whole and spit out a 3ft cube of solid compacted steel. *How*? And just as importantly, *Why*?

A Royal Reception at Huddersfield.

Eventually The Men In Blue deemed the water deep enough and we threaded our way carefully along the narrow twisting channel in the centre of the very low pound to the offending lock 6e and made our escape from the dubious delights of Milnsbridge. We were also now off the Hudderfield Narrow Canal and were, in fact, now on the Huddersfield *Broad* canal - you could be forgiven for not actually noticing a difference, to be honest, there really isn't one.

Then as we approached Kirklees College buildings we noticed that there were an unusually large number of police present - police cars and motorbikes. The canal here is a newly built section to cope with developments, and is a rather bland and narrow concrete trench through a featureless wasteland until the new lock by the college which drops the canal under the new road bridge.

The police were more or less standing around aimlessly, and a couple of the police bikers were taking a mild interest in the diversion of us operating the lock, and I asked them why all the security? Had there been an armed robbery or something?

"No, we are the security for the Duke of York who is attending a function at the college"

Me: "Oh? Which one is he then?"   This didn't go down too well. He looked totally shocked at my ignorance of our royal family and said with some exasperation "Prince Andrew." - to be honest I was still none the wiser, but thought it best not to let him know that, but I did sort of faff about a bit working the lock to see if we got a glimpse of our royal personage, and perhaps he might show an interest in our humble abode Hekla - and eventually a mob of men in posh black suit & ties came out, and totally ignored the opportunity to stop and have a chat with us. They hurried past and bundled themselves into a fleet of black Chelsea Tractors, the police bikes fired up and they all zoomed off down the road, blues & twos going like the clappers. Ah well, it was his loss.

Anyway, we had more important business to attend to than wasting our time chatting to royalty - there was a CaRT facilities block just along from there and our toilet cassette needed emptying.

Opposite the CaRT facilities is a boatyard, Appley Wharf Marina, and we were in need of a diesel top up, but it was hard to see where the diesel pump was. So we sauntered up onto the road and across the bridge into the marina office and he told us to pull across and tie up alongside the small plastic cruiser opposite us. Back to Hekla and the tricky manoeuvre to get directly from one side of the canal to the other - without trashing the plastic cruiser in the process.

We just about managed it without embarrassing ourselves *too* much, and I stepped off Hekla onto the cruiser, rope in hand, and nearly fell in. Stepping onto an 18 ton steel narrowboat has hardly any impact on the boat, a little blue and white 20ft plastic boat is like a toy by comparison and bobs about under your feet in a most alarming fashion.

We topped up the tank with 70L of diesel and we were sold a bottle of FuelSet - an additive for diesel which is supposed to sort out any water contamination - which we later decided was not so much of a problem for the likes of us, since we are Continuous Cruisers and therefore we fill our tank on a regular basis. Mainly it affects leisure boaters and perhaps those on permanent moorings when a half full tank can be left for months and condensation in the tank can lead to water contamination and also the infestation of Diesel Bug - which is a sort of algal growth in the diesel which can cause problems with blocked fuel filters, for example.

We also bought a Calder Spike since we would shortly be moving onto the Aire & Calder navigation where they have this weird paddle gear which is a wooden cog near the floor. The Calder Spike is a 3ft long 2"x4" hardwood club with a tapered and rounded end as the handle. You shove the business end into one of the holes in the floor-level cog and lever the ratchet up a bit at a time. Hard work - and Dangerous. On my second lock I tugged the resisting spike out of the hole and it whacked me on the temple. Now I know why criminals and thugs use pick axe handles as a weapon. They bloody HURT.

The next day we stayed put and took advantage of the washing machine at the marina - which involved loading up all the 'stuff' - mainly bedding and towels, for they would not fit in our little twin tub machine on Hekla - and carting them down the towpath and around a very tortuous route involving traversing a pub, a car park and the main road to get into the marina by the land lubbers entrance. (it is much easier by boat, but that would have involved a lengthy reversing manoeuvre and boats - especially ours - do not reverse in straight lines.)

And it was raining. Proper Huddersfield rain, the kind that gets you wet. We also had a flying visit from a friend from the newsgroups who lives in Huddersfield, and as usual I had no idea who he was, having never met him In Real Life before, compounded by the fact that he introduced himself by his real name. All I knew him as was JonG - At least I now know what the G stands for. Also, as is usual with these things, people who you have had many years of correspondence with *never* look like the fictional person you have built in your head.

Food and alcohol and diesel replenished, toilet emptied, water tank filled - these are all the essentials in a boating life, and we set off once more on our journey. We were now on the Huddersfield Broad canal, which has an alter-ego of Ramsdens Canal - presumably named after Harry Ramsden's famous fish & chips emporium (joke.) but first we have to negotiate the Turnbridge Loco Lift Bridge - thankfully electrically operated, which is unusual in that rather than raising at one end like a portcullis, or swinging to one side, the entire roadway is hoiked vertically up in the air to provide the headroom for boats to pass beneath. And no, I have absolutely *no idea* why is it called 'Loco Lift Bridge' - trains come no where near it.

As a mildly interesting aside, much later we picked up a 1997 vintage Nicholson Guide to the these waters and it describes the canal as an 'interesting short diversion off the main line" (of the Calder & Hebble) and recommends exploring the Narrow Canal on foot - since at that time the 'Impossible Restoration' had not happened.

So nine locks and around 3 miles finally brings us to the end of the Huddersfield/Ramsdens canal at Coopers Bridge, the last lock which drops us down onto the river Calder, with an intimidating weir immediately to the right as you exit the lock, then a short stretch to a very awkward hairpin turn onto the Calder & Hebble proper, through a flood lock, a real lock, and then, unusually, another flood lock.

By way of explanation, a Flood Lock is a lock found usually at the upstream end of a canalised section of navigable river, which are usually left open, but are closed when river levels rise too much, to prevent the artificial cuts being inundated, and also to prevent the terminally thick boater from venturing off the safety of a cut onto a raging torrent of a river in flood. It was at this 'real lock' that we had our first opportunity to use our Calder Spike, purchased not 2 days previously at Appley Wharf - and a bloody awkward contraption they are.

My log entry for the day is simply: "Long Slog. Sunshine & Showers." - and to be honest I can recall not a lot from that day. Fleeting memories of working locks, getting wet, definitely not having a fun day. We eventually moored for the night, tired - exhausted - at the first mooring opportunity we found at an un-salubrious spot called Perseverance Inn - the inn of which name had closed some while ago apparently, and it is now a private house - I do recall a basement with a light on inside all through that night (the inn/house was at road level by a bridge just behind us, and its basement was at **our** ground level - or the canal level.

The next day was a Sunday and we only moved a short distance to find a nicer mooring spot, which turned out to be by some old mine workings and an old disused colliery railway, which provided some interesting - if a little muddy - walks across the old railway bridge, along the offside and over a footbridge and back to our mooring. I then had a pleasant afternoon watching F1 on the telly and we had a relaxing day off from our labours.

Except that for reasons which escape my at the time of writing, we lifted the mattress off our bed and took a look under the boards. The bed is built in and there are 3 large storage drawers underneath it, but these are not the full width of the bed, so there is a considerable hidden storage space beyond them.

What we found was astonishing. Apart from some excess insulation boards and bits of plastic pipe there were a several of brass curtain rods - we presume from the corridor windows which had been replaced by aluminium venetian blinds (with an irritating habit of catching your arm as you sidle past them) Also a spare brass mushroom vent, and - oh the delight: A complete Cratch.

Note to the non-boater. A Cratch is a construction - usually of wood, (but some inventive boaters use all kinds of exotic and inappropriate materials) consisting of a triangular upright bit and a horizontal board which fit together at the bows to form a, well, sorry, but there is no better word than a Cratch. This is usually used as a support for a rather innovatively named Cratch Cover - basically a tent over the front well deck. In a modern narrowboat it is a kind of homage or throw-back to the old working boats which has a cratch board to support the front of the tarpaulin cargo covers. Oh sod it, here is a picture of Hekla's resplendent pinky-red cratch:

At the time we were completely underwhelmed by the contrasting colour - not to mention the, well, pinkness of it. To be fair it was originally deep red, but as any boater will tell you, red is The Worst Colour for a narrowboat because it *always* weathers badly and turns pink-ish. So after we erected it, photographed it, posted it on Facebook, we dis-assembled it again and shoved it back from whence it had come for later consideration - more of that in my subsequent new best-seller volume II (or prossibly volume III - *it depends*

Monday, and we are off once more - a whole ½ mile down Broad Cut Top Lock and at Broad Cut Bottom Lock - which drops the cut down on to the river Calder proper, the flood board was firmly in the yellow. Previously you may recall we went up the river Trent with the flood board in yellow and arrived at Cranfleet Cut to find the lock landings completely submerged - hence Lesley was adamant that we would **not** repeat that experience, so we waited to the deluge to subside a little. And as we did so a bunch of kids paddled down to the lock in canoes with a couple of adults - nominally 'in charge' and proceeded to lift the canoes out and carry them down to the lock stage on the river - larking about and shoving each other into the river, is kids are wont so to do. Then they put the canoes in the river and paddled off downstream, patently ignoring the flood warning board.

Despite my remonstration to Lesley that if the kids could do it in their little plastic canoes, Shirley our 18 ton powered narrowboat could manage, she was in 'over my dead body' mode and would brook no nonsense from me.

So we waited, and waited. Eventually a couple of hours later I could see a faint line of green on the flood board, which was enough for me to overcome Lesley's trepidations and we were off once more - Wakefield bound - for a mile until we hit Thornes flood lock, which was firmly shut. This was *not* a good spot. Lots of litter and detritus on the towpath and in the river, a very noisy construction site across from us, and plenty of graffiti were enough of a warning sign that this would not be a relaxing spot to moor for the night, but the lock gates were padlocked, so we had little choice. At least another narrowboat hove into view and we would not be alone in this urban jungle. Cold comfort, but better than facing the night horrors alone.

However the river was dropping - the board at the previous lock *had* just gone green, and after an hour or so the Men In Blue turned up and un-padlocked the flood gates to we could escape our hell-hole of a mooring.

Our New Best Friends off the other narrowboat were a little nervous about going on the river - they were time-share boaters, and this was the first time their boat pick up had been up here, so they had no experience and not a little trepidation about leaving the safety of the canal onto the wild white-water river navigations.

We, on the other hand, were seasoned river boaters. (well, we had navigated the Soar and the upper Trent during our first 3 months of life afloat) Plus we had plenty of training and experience crewing for Tony on the tidal Trent and rivers Aire, Ouse, and Derwent, so we went first out of the lock and they followed. Less than a mile downstream and the navigation takes a 90 degree right turn under a bridge, through yet another flood lock, and onto the short Wakefled cut. Miss that turn and ahead is a *massive* weir. Our past experiences did some into play her, and rather than attempt to just turn right into the cut - and get swept past it sideways in the current, we sailed majestically by, turned around mid stream and headed back against the current to make it a left turn, a much more controllable and safer manoeuvre.

Our new best friend behind us, however, had no such foresight, and kept close to the right bank and made the turn into the cut with the stream pushing them past it - but they had managed to get the bows into the cut and put the power on to ricochet off the flood lock gates and into the relative safety of the cut and its visitor moorings. When we followed in a more controlled manner and tied up, Captain Our New Best Friend said they thought we had missed the turn and had to turn around to come back. We did give them their first lesson in managing manoeuvres on a flowing river, so they appreciated that. (We think.)

Wakefield. The Hepworth Gallery. Lesley's mate from Uni. Lesley is in 7th Heaven. Phone calls were made, arrangements were made, and we were to meet James and Jade for a meal tomorrow night. Which left us with the following day to peruse the Hepworth Gallery and savour its delights (well, delights for Lesley, I myself, not having spent 3 years at Uni being instructed in the arcane skills of deciphering Modern Contemporary Fine Art, mostly gawped at 'stuff' ant tried my best to look knowledgeable and intelligent) To be fair, I do actually find some of this modern Tracy Emin type stuff more interesting than the dusty Old Masters - Art is in the Eye of the Beholder, after all, and I cannot see the fascination in an artist trying to capture a life-like image of, say, a landscape, - much simpler and quicker to take a bloody photograph.

James and Jade turned up on time and had the Grand Tour of our new home - they liked it, but 'not for us' which is a common response when people see that we live in a 7ft wide x 57ft long corridor. We walked into Downtown Wakeflield in search for a restaurant to dine in - why is it that four people can walk past and inspect *every single eatery* and *still* not decide which one to chose? To be honest I can simply not remember where or what we actually decided on that night. I *think* it was prossibly Mexican or similar, but can not say for sure. Anyway, I think we enjoyed it, and had a jolly good evening was had by all.

We spent 2 days in Wakefield - a nice enough place and the Hepworth gallery was well worth the visit, but time was pressing and we set off once more out onto the wild Aire & Calder navigation - which is a very nice stretch of river, as it happens, and the cruise to the junction with the Aire at Castleford was in bright sunshine - and excellent day after some of the deluges we had put up with in the previous few days, and it continued Set Fair all the way until we entered the Castleford Cut and moored up in the large basin just up the lock and right by the sanitary station. A bit of a high step up onto the bank, but a nice enough mooring and we explored Castleford the next day.

The entry in my spreadsheet log comments simply says: "We *Like* Castleford." The walk from the mooring took is along a riverside path to the weir which the Castleford Cut was bypassing, and a stunning gracefully curved Millennium Footbridge spanned the wide river directly over the weir, and on the far bank is an impressive old (and still functioning) flour mill with large lettering proclaiming "CASTLEFORD STONEGROUND FLOUR" I *think* it makes the flour for that bread "wi nowt teken out"

Castleford town centre proved to be an unexpected delight, with a large street market in addition to the covered market, plus lots of interesting independent shops - and bargains galore to be had. We bought a pair of heavy duty thermal lined waterproof hooded coats from one shop for the princely sum of £10 each, and I acquired a little treasure - a tiny cast scale model of a steam engine 'Adler' - I *thought* it was Stephenson's Rocket, because that is what it looks like, but there is a teeny tiny nameplate on the side saying Adler - research shows it to have actually been built by George & Robert Stephenson in 1835, but it was for Germany, and in fact was the first……. - oh sod it, here is the entry from Wikipedia:

"The Adler (German for "Eagle") was the first locomotive that was successfully used commercially for the rail transport of passengers and goods in Germany. The railway vehicle was designed and built in 1835 by the British railway pioneers George and Robert Stephenson in the English town of Newcastle. It was delivered to the Bavarian Ludwig Railway (Bayerische Ludwigsbahn) for service between Nuremberg and Fürth. It ran officially for the first time there on 7 December 1835. The Adler was a steam locomotive of the Patentee type with a wheel arrangement of 2-2-2 (Whyte notation) or 1A1

(UIC classification). The Adler was equipped with a tender of type 2 T 2."

So you get added value from this book - not only are you learning about canals, but also about the nemesis of the canal age, the railways. Anyway, the little toy train has been annoying the hell out of me ever since, as it sits on the narrow windowsill of my office - and keeps bloody falling off.   (it also appears to be a dust magnet.)

Another wonderful find in Castleford was an old fashioned hardware shop where I went in for a mooch around and asked if he had anything that might help fix a leaky coolant hose - and he pointed me at a product called "Rescue Tape" - which is basically self-amalgamating tape, (which means that when you wrap it tightly it sort of melts into itself forming a joint-free wrapping) often used by electricians to seal connectors, but this version claimed to be water and oil resistant and to withstand temperatures of well over 100 Centigrade - just to job.

The previous day's trip had not been completely uneventful, as we had a couple of mechanical issues. One was the exhaust blowing - the connection to the silencer was a bit 'iffy' and we also found that we had a water leak from an odd shaped special rubber connector to the gearbox oil cooler, which I had bodged repeatedly with silicone, insulating tape and gaffer tape. All of this would *have* to be sorted before we got to Keadby because the last thing we were going to do was venture out onto the Tidal Trent with dodgy mechanicals.

I had tracked down a replacement hose on-line, but it was being delivered to our son's house, so we would only get hold of it when we were closer, but I took the leaky hose off, cleaned away all my previous bodges of silicone, glues and tapes, and wrapped some Rescue Tape around it. When we finally got the new hose a couple of weeks later the repair had been standing up perfectly. So Rescue Tape is now an essential part of any (well this) boaters toolkit.

The second problem came to a head as we were cruising along and noticed a *lot* of smoke coming into the engine room. Fearing the worst we hurried to the bank, tied up and switched the engine off. Lifting the rear deck hatch blue-black smoke billowed out. Not Good. But the engine seemed OK. Oil OK, coolant OK, not overheating……. Then I spotted the exhaust hose was not actually connected to the silencer, and was pouring exhaust straight into the engine bay. Not only dangerous but *very* messy and everything was coated in black greasy soot.

We left things to cool down for a while (once I had painfully reminded myself that fiddling with a hot exhaust is not the best plan in the world) so we lifted all the engine boards out onto the bank and had a cup of tea. Once my cauterised fingers stopped throbbing and the engine & exhaust were at least approachable with leather work gloves I had a look at the problem - and just like a car exhaust, things tend to sort of rust-weld themselves into place. The stainless flexible exhaust hose had a 90 degree bend fitting on the end which had somehow come unscrewed off the silencer.

How it had unscrewed itself is one of life's eternal mysteries. To have unscrewed the 90 degree bend would have had to rotate quite a few turns - but the exhaust hose was still attached. Much head scratching, tongue lolling, nose picking, (no, edit that bit out.) and I attempted to disconnect the hose from the errant bent bit of pipe - and succeeded in breaking it off.

Well, at least now I had a bent pipe which I could screw back onto the exhaust without turning the flexible hose into a fair imitation of a coiled and twisted snake. But the two bits had to be joined together. With the true talent of the natural bodger I retreated to the kitchen with a pair of tin snips and rummaged a can out of the bin, cut off the other end and cut it down its length and took it back to the engine room - minor problem in that I had one (count it) old jubilee clip of the correct size. So I somehow managed to get the thing into a semi-serviceable state with the aid of some florists wire and a lot of duct tape. We were not too far from Stanley Ferry by this time so I was hoping to find a more permanent solution there - my bodge only had to hold for an hour or so.

The sparse chandlers at Stanley Ferry did not have any flexible exhaust hose, but did have exhaust bandage - not the stuff you get for repairing car exhausts where you soak it in water and wrap it around, but sound and heat insulating material - obviously not asbestos in this day and age, but something similar. Also a couple of the correct size jubilee clips - which were bloody expensive at £2.50 each, but the bloke said they were stainless steel - so that was OK then…. I think.

So back on board and the engine/exhaust cooled down enough not to cauterise my skin on contact, the initial bodge was redone with the two expensive stainless steel jubilee clips, another cut open tin can, and the whole assembly wrapped around with the aforementioned exhaust tape with some florists wire holding it all in place. I can happily report that this particular bodge is still holding up as I type this 2 years later.

The Final Stretch

I can tell this is the final stretch because I am using the Nicholson's maps to plot our journey and it has just helpfully said *<continued in Book 6>* which meant we were leaving the North West & Pennines and entering the Nottingham, York and North East waters - which includes our destination, the tidal Trent and West Stockwith lock onto the Chesterfield canal.

We left Castleford mid afternoon and now we were on sort-of familiar waters, as we had crewed for Tony on Dreamcatcher a couple of year previously from Whitley Bridge to Castleford. It had been an 'interesting' cruise that one - with a couple of highly questionable detours. First was the Ferrybridge Power Station, and the old Coal Barge unloading dock.

Tom Puddings were the name given to trains of small rectangular barges filled with coal at collieries and towed by a tug to Goole. At either end of this route were ingenious constructions which lifted the little barges bodily out of the water, and tipped them over to empty the coal directly into coastal ships. The unloading dock at Ferrybridge is a very impressive structure with a channel between the bank and a large pier in the river. These barges were bigger than the Tom Puddings. Below is a composite image taken from a video we shot of the adventure.

The second was an irresistible side cutting which Tony steered us into which turned out to be an old colliery loading wharf, like a little marina off the river Aire. Once inside we tied up for a look around and *then* we saw the sign - the usual list of stuff that is forbidden - cycling, swimming etc. but including "No Powered Craft" - which was a bit daft as you can only see this edict once you have sailed into the place.

It was also on this trip that we were going around a bend in the river to be confronted by the Humber Princess - the huge inland oil tanker steaming towards us on *our* side of the river. We weren't going to argue with him about the finer points of inland navigation - but thankfully the skipper saw us and moved aside before ramming us and sending us to whatever the river equivalent is of Davy Jones's Locker.

We had no such worries ourselves on this trip as the commercial traffic on the Aire had ceased - the tankers were not up to modern safety standards and the coal was now all transported by road - which is a bit bloody stupid if you ask me, because barges must be a lot cheaper and more efficient at moving such bulk cargoes.

We moored for the night at Nottingley and treated ourselves to a pint at the Steam Packet Inn on the canalside there, and the next day we continued on the final push to the Trent at Keadby. Although this stretch of the navigation is mostly arrow-straight and wide, it is not unattractive. At Southfield Junction we took a sharp right turn onto the New Junction Canal - one of the last canals to be built in England, and arrow-straight for 5.1/2 miles - broken only by several large and thankfully electric/hydraulically operated lift bridges, and the huge Sykehouse Lock, which is a bit complicated, having a swing bridge across the middle of it.

You have to go to the control panel and insert the key - then *carefully* read the instructions, which tell you to go and open the swing bridge across the middle of the lock - this one manual - then go back and press the button to drain the lock, then the button to open the bottom gates, then close the gates, then the button to re-fill the lock, then to open the top gates, then to close the top gates, then to close the swing bridge, lower the barriers - then, and only then, will the control panel release its vice-like grip on your key. The next time we used this lock it all went horribly wrong - but that story is for the next edition.

The New Junction ends at an acutely angled junction where it continues straight on as the River Don navigation and on to the terminus at Sheffield, or a hairpin left turn onto the Stainforth and Keadby Canal - which was the way we were going. This is another relatively 'modern' canal, but is a mix of straight and curly bits as it traverses New Holland (the name for this area of flatland in South Yorkshire).

We moored up for the night in a very pleasant rural spot just short of Thorne, at what turned out to be an old colliery site - now grassed over and made into yet another 'county park' - a sad end to a once large and proud British industry.

Finally on to Thorne and we moored on the pontoons in the fenced and gated secure CaRT visitor moorings there, and our 2 sons Ross & Michael came along to see us, and brought the new hose that I had ordered on-line. We also called in to the excellent Thorne Marine chandlery there.

A proper old fashioned chandlery with lots of proper boaty and engine stuff, unlike some which are mainly filled with bling and expensive equipment and fittings to make life perfect for the modern shiny-boater. Here I bought a new fan belt and a spare as well as an engine air filter. Ross was only to please to get his hands dirty and change the frayed fan belt and fit the air filter for me - he is an odd cove in that way, he loves messing about with anything mechanical - but I am not complaining. Oh no.

We left Thorne and carried on to Keadby and our first time solo on the Tidal Trent. We had done it several times with Tony in recent years, so we knew what to expect and what to do, but when it is your own boat & home and you don't have someone with decades of experience with you, even the most cold-hearted boater will have some worries to play on the mind. Before that, however, we were moored at Keadby and our friend Mal Nicholson was at home on his restored Humber Super Sloop 'Spider T'

I was surprised to find that Mal had never been on a narrowboat in his life. Well, I had never been on a Humber Super Sloop in *my* life either, so I suppose I shouldn't be surprised. Anyway, we gave Mal the grand tour, then our sons arrived - trailing problems as usual.

Apparently Mike's cars alternator had given up the ghost. However he had a *huge* 200Ah truck battery in the boot - to power the bloody huge sub-woofer in his sound system - yes, Mike was one of those people who drive past you in the street and you can hear them a mile off from the boom-boom-boom of their 'music' (and I use the term loosely)

Anyway, he and Ross had wired this monster up to the car's 'normal' battery and were driving on that. They were a bit unsure that it had enough charge left to get them home, so Mal had a look at it - but could not find an easy fix other than a new alternator, which were not exactly abundant in Keadby at 5:00 p.m. on a damp Saturday evening, so we got our small generator out and set it to charging while Mal invited all 4 of us for a guided tour of Spider T - which, if you have never seen it, is bloody impressive inside. A cast iron spiral staircase leads down from the deck into a large open plan main salon with kitchen area sporting a large AGA sold fuel stove, and lots and lots of polished mahogany setting off the deep red Chesterfield styles seating around the walls and the huge polished mahogany dining table dominating the room. You can see and read all abut Spider T on the website www.spidert.co.uk

Ross & Mike said their goodbyes and left with our generator in the boot so that, should the worse happen, they could at least recharge that giant battery from the gennies 12v supply. Then Mal invited over to Spider T for a drink, and we spent a very convivial evening with Mal and his wife Tracy - and got quite, quite drunk while putting a dent into Mal's wine cellar.

Mal and Tracy were living on Spider T at the time, since their home and business had been flooded out by and exceptional spring tide surge the previous December. Mal has a business Trentside Classics which specialises in Alfa Romeos and other Italian exotica and has an enviable collection of rare motors, including a Ferarri F1 car and The Duchess - a Ferrari Dino, as well as an Alfa Montreal 'supercar' with an Alfa F1 engine - and these were all flooded as well. If you ever have the good fortune to meet with Mal, whatever you do don't raise the subject of insurance companies. You could be there for hours listening to Mal's (justifiable) ranting. ;^)

We eventually staggered back to Hekla and settled down to bed ready (or not) for tomorrows trip down the tidal Trent to our destination of West Stockwith.

If you are ever in a position to take a boat onto rivers - especially tidal stretches, then it is imperative to talk to the lock keepers and take heed of their expert advice. The previous evening we had just caught Mark, one of the three Keadby lock keepers and arranged our passage down the lock for 8:00 a.m. the next morning, when another lock keeper, Mark, was on duty. Rather confusingly all three Keadby lock keepers are named Mark. Little Mark, Mark 2 and Big Mark, just so you know for future reference. It was Mark 2 that we arranged things with the previous day, and it was Big Mark who was on duty that morning. There was also another narrowboat, Genevieve who were also travelling down with us at the same time.

Big Mark assured us that they were letting us out onto the river with the incoming tide which would speed us on our way upstream to West Stockwith, where we should arrive at the peak of the tide, or 'slack water' to make our entrance into the lock at West Stockwith so much easier.

So with much trepidation we made the lock transit on a bright and sunny May morning and turned South heading upstream with incoming the tide. We let Genevieve go in front, and settled down for what turned out to be a very pleasant morning's cruise down the wide river. The first sight you have is of Guiness Wharf on the opposite bank, where there is usually at least one or two coastal ships loading or unloading there, then you pass under the impressive large steel lift bridge carrying the main road from Scunthorpe across the river, then a little further on you pass under the M62 motorway with the cars and lorries looking like dinky toys passing high overhead.

The river snakes its way South from Trent Falls where it merges with the Yorkshire Ouse into the Humber Estuary, passing twin villages on either bank. Allthorpe and Burringham, then East Butterwick and West Butterwick, followed by Owston Ferry where you can see old riverside warehouses, opposite East Ferry, looking very picturesque in the bright May sunshine. The basic rule of river navigation is to always keep to the outside on bends, which is where the river flow scours the channel, whilst the inside of bends tend to be shallow where sediment gets deposited. There are excellent river guides available which have the channels and 'sunken islands' identified for you to help you make a safe passage.

There was no wind, the river surface was like a millpond - but appearances can be deceptive. I have a speed app on my smartphone which uses GPS to give an accurate measure of your *actual* speed as opposed to your speed through the water. We had Hekla on just above tickover, which equates to around 2mph on normal canals - but the phone was telling us we were actually travelling at *Eleven Knots*.

One quite essential piece of kit for rivers is a short wave radio - you can get away with a mobile phone, but radio's are somehow more comforting and they make you feel like a 'proper' sailor. We heard our little hand-held Cobra unit crackle into life and:

"West Stockwith, West Stockwith, this is narrowboat Genevieve, Narrowboat Genevieve, Over"

"NB Genevieve, NB Genevieve, West Stockwith Receiving you, Over"

"West Stockwith, West Stockwith, NB Genevieve, we are about half a mile downstream, how is the lock set?"

"NB Genevieve, NB Genevieve, this is West Stockwith, the lock is set for you and the gates are open, you should be able to just come straight in"

Riiigght. - we were *still* cracking on a pace, the tide was still taking us with it, no where near 'slack water'. We hung back as best we could as Genevieve, taking the locky at his word, made a right turn into the lock entrance - and sailed majestically past it sideways.

West Stockwith has to be the most awkward river/canal lock on the system. The Trent, previously imposingly wide, suddenly narrows and makes a sharp left turn just where the lock is. The narrows and bend combine to speed up the flow alarmingly, and it is an absolute *sod* of a job in anything but slack water or a very mild flow.

We held back as Genevieve managed to complete her inadvertent turn and re-approach the lock from upstream against the current, which gives you *much* better control of the boat, and the just managed to make the turn into the safety of the lock. We cruised straight past the lock entrance and turned ourselves around upstream and battled the still very strong current back to the lock entrance. We were on full power to make headway against the tide, probably doing around 1 or 2 mph at revs that would see us travelling at 6 mph on still, deep water. This is where I let myself get the better of myself, as the locky, seeing the strength of the current, and the difficulties Genevieve had offered for us to come along side the bank the they would warp us into the lock with ropes.

I was having none of that. Our mate Tony has been a good instructor on our various river trips with him, and I was confident I could make it under our own power. So I told the locky we "would be OK, thanks" and went for it.

I would *like* to say that everything went text-book perfect - and it did - up to a point, that point being when the front half of Hekla was into the lee of the lock approach wall and released from the clutches of the tide pushing her backwards, and promptly shot forward into the lock wall at a quite acute angle.

So we sort of ricocheted our way into West Stockwith - ignoring the sounds of breaking glass coming from inside Hekla.

We had Arrived. With a BANG it has to be said, but on the 19th May we had finally reached our destination on the Chesterfield Canal Had we waited in Nottingham for Holme Lock to be repaired and open we would have probably arrived on the same day.

Looking at our maiden voyage using the excellent Canalplan web site, had we set off from Norbury and taken the normal route it would have been 149 miles and 51 locks in under 14 days. We had *actually* done some *650* miles, *441* locks in 4 months.

Our journey wasn't finished though. As we discovered, moorings on the Chesterfield are not that plentiful. The basin was full, as was the canal itself immediately beyond the basin - apart from places where it was too shallow or weed grown to get to the side, so we continued on for another 6 miles and 4 locks until we finally found a place to moor up just past Drakeholes Tunnel.

The whole experience was thoroughly enjoyable - even the bad bits. The cold wet slog up the Pennines to the Harecastle, our first night on the boat, cruising to Chester and mooring under the city walls, the contrasts between remote rural idylls and urban post-industrial landscapes. One thing we learned was that our original Plan A - which was to base ourselves in the East Midlands because of my customers was not necessary, because I could work perfectly well from anywhere with a decent 3G internet signal, so the entire canal system is open to us to explore.

Before Drakeholes we passed a little 23ft Norman Cruiser which had broken down. We later bought that boat off the owners for £1 - but, dear reader, you will have to be patient and wait for the next instalment before you learn about that little episode - and the fact that once we had arrived at our intended 'home cruising grounds' things didn't *quite* go to plan and we would have to turn around and re-trace our steps back over to the West side of the country.

Appendix (a)

A note on spelling, grammar, punctuation, syntax, and other such irrelevances.

Despite initial appearances, this book **has** been proof read. The appearance of odd words or phrases that may jar with the grammar polizei, such as 'prossibly'[0] are present with the full intent (mostly) of the author.

I must confess to having been unduly influenced by spending *far* too much time on a certain Usenet Newsgroup Alt.Rec.Sheds which is populated by a motley assortment of weirdo's where language and grammar are treated with a gay cavalier abandon, and has its very own dictionary and usage evolved over many years of collective torturing of English as she is spoke.

For example, swearing is heavily frowned upon, and swear words are usually coded using ROT13 (the first 13 letters of the alphabet are transposed with the second 13 letters - Oh sod it, just go to www.rot13.com and it will do it for you)

Included in the loosely defined term of swear words are words (or worms) which may offend the sensibilities of those of us who prefer not to mix jbex[42] with pleasure. Units of measurement are equally arcane, and time is measured in fortnights, length in furlongs, volume in firkins (a calculator and conversion tables may cumin andy at this point), thus an hour is 0.003 fortnights (roughly) and at the time of writing my age is 1486[21] fortnights (roughly)

Sometimes words(worms) are simply mis-spelled, just for the hell of it, or because it amuses small minds, and it also please to encrypt some common phrases for simla reasons, e.g. 'Mind You' can become 'mined ewe' or even in extremis 'excavated sheep'

Another tactic often used to bewilder the unwary is BudyCript - named after an early member of The Shed who's name was not, as you would expect (or not) Budy, but his surname was Budd. Buddycript is the simple expedient of speeling worms with all the correct letters, but not *necessarily* in the correct order.

This is especially useful on the internet where by diverse and devious means $Megacorp$ spy on all and sundry and pounce on any mention of their name to be exploited by the demons in marketing, thus when referencing a shop (or siop if you prefer the welshish worm) the name will usually be budycripted, e.g. eTsoc, dAsa, or otherwise obfusticated such as sins berries, weight rose - you get the picture. (or if not, perhaps put this tomb back where you found it)

Just Because, OK?

[0] A mongrel worm made up of Probably and Possibly - who says I am indecisive?
[42] jbex = w*rk x rot13
[21] as it happens, the year Agrippa von Nettesheim[53], German occultist/alchemist/royal astrologer was born (or died, one or t'other)
[53] No, I have no idea either.

Appendix (b)

The Politics Of The Canals

<Caveat> - similarities to people In Real Life are purely unintentional and/or coincidental, so don't blame me, OK?

We had read on various forums and in canal magazine letters pages about some people's attitudes to Continuous Cruisers - mostly small minded tick-box people who invariably come out with the phrase "Not paying your fair share" - meaning we did not pay for a mooring - which in most cases the money goes to a marina company, with only a small percentage going to CaRT.

There is a lot of politics in the canal community - far more than we thought before we moved onto Hekla. I suppose it is like land-based society, but more compact and because of the constant movement you tend to mix it with other groups far more than if you lived in a house on a nice tidy suburban housing estate where you may occasionally have the odd neighbourly conflict, but on the cut you never know who your neighbours are going to be from one mooring to the next.

There are many types on the canal:
The Traditionalist - usually with a restored old working boat or a pretend old working boat with fake rivets and an old engine, say a Russell Newbury or an old Lister - mostly these are 'hobby' boaters and are usually seen with a flat cap, braces, waistcoat, boots and with a can of Brasso in one hand.

The Leisure Boater - generally has a mooring in a marina somewhere, quite often has a bright shiny new boat - which is cherished as a possession - but all sorts of people and boats fit into this group and the true enthusiast may have anything from an old 30ft Springer to a brand shiny new Tim Tyler design, and in all states of repair. The most difficult to categorise in terms of type of person, because they can be open friendly gregarious types, and there can also be stuck-up snobs (like the ones at Braunston Locks who didn't want to share with us)

Then you have the Time Share and Hire boaters. Time Shares are often the worst offenders when it comes to speeding past moored boats, because they are usually 'on a mission' to cover as many lock-miles as they can in their allotted 2 weeks. Hire boaters are an eclectic lot, ranging from complete novices who are eager to learn, but can be a right nuisance at times, to serial hirers who are canal enthusiasts who can not manage a boat of their own, nor want to be tied to a time-share contract.

Finally you have the Live Aboards - again an eclectic mix of people of all ages and types. There are live aboards with a residential mooring who mainly treat their boats as a sort of floating bungalow, which they can take out every so often, say of a weekend when they might cruise a few miles to a favourite canal side pub, get drunk, then return 'home' the next day.

There are live aboards who do not have a mooring, like ourselves, who are termed 'continuous cruisers'. We mostly like the freedom to move when and where we please. We have restrictions, generally speaking we can moor anywhere for up to 14 days, provided there are not signed time limits, then we have to move somewhere else. (we have managed at most 11 days in one spot before getting bored and moving on)

Then there are the live aboards with no home mooring, but with ties to a specific area, such as a job or school for their kids. There is an increase in this type of boater, who mostly see a boat as cheap housing - there are concentrations of them in and around London and on the Kennet and Avon canal's Western end near Bath and Bristol. These are the boaters who can cause problems for people like ourselves as continuous cruisers, because they annoy a great many other boaters, and have earned the nickname 'Continuous Moorers' or 'Bridge Hoppers'

We have nothing against these people at all, and I know a lot of other canal people don't have a problem either, but there is a very vocal minority, the sort who write in to the Canal Press in Green Ink denouncing these people as a disgrace, a blight on their lives, hogging all the best moorings, and above all Not Paying Their Fair Share.

The conditions laid down for Boaters Without A Home Mooring were laid down in acts of parliament, the most relevant of which was passed in 1995, and the relevant section for us Continuous Cruisers is as follows:

"the applicant for the relevant consent satisfies the Board that the vessel to which the application relates will be used bona fide for navigation throughout the period for which the consent is valid without remaining continuously in any one place for more than 14 days or such longer period as is reasonable in the circumstances."

This is pretty vague, and was made intentionally so to allow for a high degree of flexibility in the interpretation and enforcement, however there are a group of the Green Ink brigade who are not satisfied with 'Vague' nor 'Flexible' and keep demanding 'Clarification', for example what, exactly, constitutes " *bona fide for navigation*"?

Clearly a boat moored at point A for 14 days, which then moves to point B a couple of hundred yards away, then in 14 days moves *back* to point A is not quite entering into the spirit of things.

CaRT have repeatedly tried to define this, the latest being trying to define a 'place' and also that A to B to A is not acceptable. 'Place' is a difficult one, and various definitions have been applied over time, but the latest is that the boat should go from A to B to C at least, and that this journey should cover a minimum of 20 Kilometres.

All it boils down to is this: It Takes All Sorts. No matter what type of boater a person is, ultimately we are all in a community with (mostly) a love of canals and rivers and boats and history and nature and scenery and ..... well, you get the picture.

We all mostly get on with each other far better than most land based communities. In the main boaters are a fabulous bunch of people who will always be prepared to go the extra mile to help another boater.

As an example of this community spirit there was an old lady and her dog who had become homeless through no fault of her own - Modern Britain, don't you love it? - and she was sleeping rough along the Macclesfield Canal. The owner/operators local fuel boat discovered her plight and determined to do something about it. They knew of a tiny (20ft) abandoned boat nearby, and they approached CaRT with a proposal that they would license and insure it if they could have it for free - CaRT agreed and they did a very good job of renovating this little boat and presented it to the homeless lady (and her dog) - and she now lives on her new little floating home, cosy and warm and above all safe.

So the next time you are gongoozling by a lock on a canal near you and you see a single handed boater working the lock, please, please, offer to help them - if only to close the gates as they leave to save them having to tie up and walk back to do it themselves. Ask first, of course, because some people do actually prefer to do it themselves, but the vast majority will thank you for you kindness, and you will feel a warm glow inside from helping a fellow human being. You never know, you might even enjoy it so much that you become an official CaRT volunteer lock keeper. Or even, dare I say it, become bitten by 'the bug' and get into boating yourself. It is also good exercise. In the preceding [0] 2 - 300 pages I myself dropped 2 waist sizes - my most used tool was a hole punch to keep adding holes to my trouser belt.

[0] Well, not in writing these pages, obviously, but in the adventures we had described within them.

Printed in Great Britain
by Amazon

65671977R00097